Namasté

INITIATION AND TRANSFORMATION

A HOW-TO FOR THOSE WHO WISH TO EMBRACE ASOUL

© 1997

(handwritten inscription: To Tanya & Tom, For all the support and encouragement you've given me. Soar like an Eagle. Joyce A Kovelman)

Joyce A. Kovelman
Ph.D. Anatomy, Ph.D. Psychology

J

JALMAR PRESS
Carson, California

Namasté: Initiation and Transformation

A how-to for those who wish to embrace ASOUL

Copyright © 1998 by Joyce A. Kovelman, Ph.D. Anatomy, Ph.D. Psychology

Jalmar Press
Permissions Dept.
24426 S. Main St., Suite 702
Carson, CA 90745
(310)816-3085 Fax (310)816-3092
E-mail: blwjalmar@worldnet.att.net

Library of Congress Cataloging-in-Publication Data

Kovelman, Joyce Ann.
 Namasté: initiation and transformation   A how-to for those who
wish to embrace ASOUL / by Joyce A. Kovelman.
  p. cm.
 Companion volume to Once upon ASOUL.
 Includes bibliographical references.
 ISBN 1-880396-53-X
  1. Spiritual life—Miscellanea. 2. Self-actualization
(Psychology)—Miscellanea.   I. Title.
BF1999.K69   1997
291.4—dc21   97-25567
                                                   CIP

25+YEARS
AWARD WINNING
PUBLISHER
𝓟

Published by Jalmar Press

Namasté: Initiation and Transformation

Author: Joyce A. Kovelman, Ph.D. Anatomy, Ph.D. Psychology
Editor: Susan Remkus
Project Director: Jeanne Iler
Production
  & Design: Electronic Publishing Services, Inc.

Manufactured in the United States of America

10 9 8 7 6 5 4 3 2 1
ISBN: 1-880396-53-X

Dedicated to the Awakening Spirit

ACKNOWLEDGMENTS

The same people who so ably and generously lent support and assistance to the writing of my first book, have also helped with the writing and publication of *Namasté: Initiation and Transformation*. Special thanks to Andrea Cagan, my editor and friend, for her gracious and gentle support. I am indebted to Susan Herner for her suggestion that I write a book which encourages action and empowerment, and brings heaven down to earth. The love and encouragement I received from Lil and Roy Griffiths nourished me throughout this endeavor. Sarah Minden listened to my ideas with the willingness of an angel, while Elizabeth Caulder and Carolina Loren gave endless encouragement.

Susan Tereba has an amazing ability to translate story and myth into emotion and art. She has been an incredible friend and inspiration. Heartfelt appreciation to my publisher, Dr. Bradley Winch, Sr., of Jalmar Press, for all his help and expertise, and to Susan Remkus for her outstanding job of copy editing.

My family has stood steadfast throughout the long months of writing, editing and publishing. Without their encouragement, support, and love, I would not have fulfilled this dream. My husband, Gilbert; children, Paul, Robert, Bruce, Gabrielle, Alexandra, Noreen and Angela; and grandaughters, Breeana and Catherine, continually nurtured and replenished my Spirit. Thank you, thank you, thank you...

I am deeply indebted to the friends, teachers, and colleagues, too many to mention by name, who willingly read portions of Namasté and offered wonderful insights, suggestions, and assistance. To all who helped me journey the Path of the Heart, I humbly say, "Thanks."

Last, but not least, heartfelt gratitude to Mother Earth and Father Sky.

My special thanks to Bryan and to Jeanne.

TABLE OF CONTENTS

SECTION FIVE

Creating a New Path   **65**

PREFACE

Namasté was born out of a need to bring heaven down to earth, and a desire to encourage people to live their dreams, hopes, and visions in our everyday world. My goal in writing Namasté is to empower people by providing the tools and techniques that enable readers to fulfill their visions and their highest potential.

Namasté speaks to readers who wish to change and to grow; it is a guide, a map, and a path to enlightenment and self-realization. Since Namasté recognizes the uniqueness of each reader, it refrains from offering a rigid schedule or formulary. There is no single regimen that will enable everyone to reach enlightenment. Rather, Namasté offers an array and assortment of ideas, tools, and techniques to assist and enhance change. Readers are invited to freely select and choose the ideas and practices that work best for them. Namasté empowers the reader, not the author(ity) out there. I encourage readers to trust their inner wisdom and intuition and let their inner Self be their guide.

As a Psychologist, I have learned that the process of self-actualization is never ending. The first step is to recognize the need for change and behaving differently. Without this recognition, nothing is likely to happen. So we begin by accepting and acknowledging where we are in the present moment. The second step is to venture into the inner spaces, in order to gain the awareness and insight necessary for personal transformation. We must change our inner Selves before we can change the world—out there. Once we take responsibility for our own behavior, beliefs, attitudes, and ideas, we are ready to begin.

In many ways, the third step is the hardest. This step requires the determination and willingness to change. A strong intention is necessary if we are to reach our goals. Without motivation to change, we will gradually get tired, give up, and stop trying to move beyond the obstacles in our path. The willingness to grow flows from the inside-out. Motivation always empowers, and empowerment leads to action and transformation.

Lastly, I have refrained from calling Namasté a work-book. I believe that most of us work too hard and too much. We work out in the gym, we work in the garden, we work at our tennis score, we work at work, and so on. Indeed, too many of us work until we drop, while still others have no work to do at all. Namasté reveals that inner balance and harmony are necessary in order to heal our Selves, our families, and our world.

Namasté invites you to begin the inner journey on the Path of the Heart and to re-connect with Spirit and the sacred dimensions of Soul. Namasté encourages you to journey more deeply into your own being, to grow more aware, and to participate in the process of creation, itself.

INTRODUCTION

Namasté is a Sanskrit word which means the divinity within me honors and respects the divinity within you. Namasté reminds us that all existence is endowed with a spark of the Divine. We are all born with good intent, a yearning to fulfill our higher potential, and a psychic map to point the way. *Our mission* is to grow and evolve in ways uniquely our own.

Most of us constantly reduce substance and form to ever smaller components. We do so in order to understand more fully how things work or how they are made. Scientists seek to understand the properties and characteristics of matter, seeking the fundamental building blocks that give rise to all matter. Similarly, psychologists have reduced the psyche into more manageable, understandable component parts and inner selves. Even spiritual traditions evoke the blessings of gods and goddesses and other deities that bear striking resemblances to humankind. Everything has become so complicated and overwhelming; we want someone else, out there, to tell us how, or to provide us a map of the way. No wonder self-help and how-to manuals line our bookshelves. In truth, we want to feel strong and in control.

All too often, we mistake the map for the journey, and fail to consciously embrace our individual paths and our destinies. Each of us has an innate knowing, a unique psychic map designed just for us, which unfolds as we live out our days and years upon earth. Unfortunately, many do not realize that maps already exist to guide our way.

Those who remember, as well as those already growing and awakening, tell us what is possible. The destinations of SOUL are known. Your own unique map dwells deep within your heart and psyche. Everyone is endowed with sparks of the Divine.

Namasté's special message speaks to your inborn propensities for growth, actualization, and transformation. Aware that no one can travel another's path, Namasté provides an array of possibilities, ideas, tools, and pathways for you to explore. There is no "right way" or "one pathway" to travel. There are only your way, my way, his way, and her way. Namasté is a path to wholeness and serenity for those ready to make their own decisions, take responsibility for their choices, trust their intuitions, reach for their higher potential, and allow their inner wisdom to unfold.

Deep within your heart and psyche reside the blueprints that SOUL has already bestowed upon you. You must look within to find them. Listen quietly, and you will hear their message. Honoring your intuition and feelings allows your own wisdom to unfold. Namasté echos Spirit's call, urging us to embrace SOUL and to discover the One We Are.

The pathway towards wholeness is not without difficulty and risk. A wise traveler prepares Self and psyche for the many stages of this journey, ensuring safety and completion of ASelf's purpose in this lifetime.

Namasté, companion book to *Once Upon ASOUL,* translates ideas and principles into everyday solutions and exercises. It offers tools of initiation and transformation. Namasté simultaneously speaks to the many levels and dimensions of personhood. Using exercises, stories, and guided visualizations, Namasté gently encourages you to begin your daily practices.

Most workbooks and manuals like to tell you how, when, why, and what to do. Even though you have never personally met any of the authors, they still insist that they know what is good for you. Instead, Namasté recognizes that each of us is capable of making our own choices and setting our own goals. We can safely trust Psyche's wisdom and rhythms. Namasté gently encourages everyone to take charge of his or her destiny.

This book can be read sequentially, one topic following the next. However, I encourage you to enjoy it in a non-linear fashion. As you intuitively open to any section or page, certain issues and subjects will appear to jump from the page, inviting further exploration and practice. Others prefer to be savored and contemplated later. Let your intuition help you decide where to begin.

Continuous use of Namasté bestows gifts of personal growth and transformation. I hope you will read it often. As you evolve, your experience of Namasté also evolves. Reader and map magically unfold together; Self and SOUL joyously unite.

Five sections are included in NAMASTÉ:

1. Implications for our community and our world.

2. The process of transformation.

3. Goals for the Self.

4. Techniques and methods to achieve our goals.

5. Creating a new path.

Namasté forges a sacred bridge between inner and outer realities, and helps us transform passive dialogue about our values into compassionate action and change. We become more caring, sensitive, and loving people, consciously healing our Selves, our families, our communities, and our world. Namasté reminds us that humanity connects heaven and earth. The awesome responsibility to create a brave new world and a compassionate specieshood is ours. We are the gods emerging. Let us begin.

CAST OF CHARACTERS

Whenever you begin a journey, it is a good idea to take a map or guide along with you. They make your journey easier and your way less hazardous. Maps guide your journey, enabling you to reach your desired destination. The book's essential definitions are found in the Cast of Characters.

ALL THAT IS: ABSOLUTE, ATMAN, CREATOR, DIVINE, GOD, NUMINOUS, SPIRIT, and SOURCE.

APSYCHE: Also called the Mind. Totality of All psychic processes, conscious and unconscious. PSYCHE is the messenger between Soul and all other levels and dimensions of Selfhood (manifest and unmanifest).

ASELF: Earthly personality and heroine of *Once Upon ASOUL*. She/He is a fictitious character who dwells in the world of space-time and matter. ASELF is a variation of Me and you.

ASOUL: ASELF's Soul, personalized for purposes of our story. Determines major life challenges and events that ASELF will experience in the world of physicality. Has endowed ASELF with free will and choice. ASOUL seeks to unite with ASELF so that their goals and needs become one.

FIGURE 1   Multi-Dimensional Selfhood

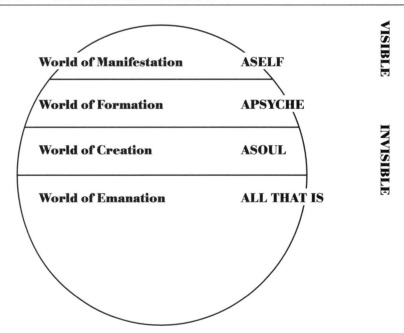

An iceberg provides a useful metaphor for the circle above. Over 80% of this enormous glacier is submerged beneath sea-level. Similarly, only the manifest portion of our multi-faceted, multi-leveled, multi-dimensional SELFHOOD appears in the world of physicality. The rest of our SELF remains invisible and hidden in the non-material realms of Spirit. All portions of SELF are part of the Whole and the One We Are.

IMPLICATIONS FOR OUR COMMUNITY AND OUR WORLD

CRISIS: DANGER AND OPPORTUNITY

The patriarchal, reductionist paradigm of the last two to three millennia, the time since the Fall from Paradise, is coming to an end. We are approaching critical mass and chaos as well as the end of an age. We are scared and there is no place we can hide. We call out for change, but shake and flee when it arrives. We live in a most auspicious and historic time, one fraught with rich possibilities as well as great peril.

The Chinese, many millennia ago, recognized that at least two different states existed side by side within any crisis. They understood that every crisis is actually a moment of probability and uncertainty, with one probability leading to danger and possible disaster, the other espousing solution and resolution. This concept is also fundamental to recently proposed scientific theories of chaos and complexity.*

What will happen? I do not know with any more certainty than anyone else. Despite my fears and concerns, I believe that each of us can make a difference in the potential healing of our world and our society. Every change is amplified

---

*For a more detailed definition of the Chinese understanding of "Crisis," please refer to *Once Upon ASOUL,* Section Two.

and multiplied as it flows through an open system. Collectively, such changes are further multiplied and amplified. We can make an impact! Never has it been more critical to act. To procrastinate is to miss a window of opportunity still open to humankind. To change the world, you must first change your Self.

One way we can help humanity reclaim and embrace its spirituality is to form a global community which honors all forms of Consciousness and life upon earth. This means that no species or individual has the right to gain at the expense of another. A spiritual humanity demands the end of war and violence. Indeed, there are no holy wars! We are all GOD stuff. SPIRIT infuses all matter. It is no longer possible to consider our planetary problems in terms of ethnic, national, or racial priorities. An "us vs. them" or the "have vs. the have nots" mentality is an obstacle to real peace and happiness.

Our concerns must shift to embrace one humanity and to respect all of existence. Each of us is invited to rejoin the sacred circle and to forge a global community. It is only through collective effort that we will survive. If earth perishes, we all perish!

Joseph Campbell echoed these thoughts in the following passage,

"The world as the center of the universe, the world divided from the heavens, the world bound by horizons in which love is reserved for the members of the in group: that is the world that is passing away. Apocalypse does not point to a fiery Armageddon but to the fact that our ignorance and our complacency are coming to an end."[1]

The physical world faithfully reflects the ills and challenges within the human psyche. It points the way humankind must change and develop to enhance its likelihood for survival. We are becoming aware of the imbalances in our environment, of our need to sustain our precious rain-forests, and the urgent necessity to stop polluting land, air, and sea if we wish to sustain life. Stringent, life-sustaining laws are necessary in order to prevent toxic dumps and spills, as well as pollution of soil and waterways. In the same way, we need to stop polluting our own bodies with drugs, alcohol, additives, preservatives, too much sugar, too much salt, and too much of everything. Our polluted immune systems cry out for help, no longer able to breathe our dirty air, and less able to heal our bodies of chronic fatigue syndrome, AIDS, asthma, cancer, and other auto-immune diseases that signal the breakdown of body and Soul.

Wangari Matthai poignantly agrees,

"If we lived a life that valued and protected trees, it would be a life that also valued and protected us—and gave us great joy. A way of life that kills trees, our present way of life, kills us too, body and soul."[2]

And a proverb from Kenya reminds us,

> "Treat the earth well... it was not given to you by your parents. ... It was lent to you by your children."[3]

The growing number of homeless people warns that soon humanity will become a homeless species if we do not heal Mother Earth and work in partnership with nature. Our clogged freeways and turnpikes reflect our clogged arteries and rising blood pressures. The escalation of violence indicates the increased self-hatred we feel and project outwardly. The growing abuse of our nation's women and children reveals our fear and terror of the feminine aspects within our psyches. The following Chinese poem illustrates the oppression, disdain, and repression of the Psyche's feminine aspect, as long ago as the third century:

> "How sad it is to be a woman.
> Nothing on earth is held so cheap.
> Boys stand leaning at the door
> Like Gods fallen out of heaven.
> Their hearts brace the Four Oceans.
> The wind and dust of a thousand miles.
> No one is glad when a girl is born:
> By her the family sets no store."[4]

It is spiritually necessary to restore and honor the feminine aspects of the human psyche if we are to grow into our fullest potential as individuals, and realize inner and outer peace. Feminine consciousness is part of both the male and the female psyche. Feminine, in partnership with Masculine, offers the ability and insight to restore sanity to our world, enabling humankind to survive. I know of no other species that batters its women and kills its children. The escalating number of victims of abuse and rape is staggering! Indeed, Pope John has assailed the "Culture of Death" that pervades our world.

Jennifer and Roger Woolger agree,

> "Our whole culture—with its endless violence, homeless people on the streets, colossal nuclear arsenals, and global pollution—is sick. It is sick because it is out of harmony with itself; it suffers from what the Hopi Indians call koyaanisqatsi, which is rendered in English, 'crazy life, life in turmoil, life out of balance.' What is missing is the feminine dimension in our spiritual and psychological lives; that deep mystical sense of the earth and her cycles and of the cosmos as a living mystery. We have lost our inner connection to that momentous power that used to be called the Great Mother of us all."[5]

Without the feminine, the human psyche finds itself without the resources, wisdom, and gnosis to heal Self and world. The implosion of our economy signals and reflects the implosion of our own individual resources. Our populations swell even as our natural resources decline, further draining our reserves and stressing our economies, our political institutions, our families, and our tempers. Inwardly, there is a corresponding population explosion of inner Selves and sub-personalities causing many of us to feel fragmented and broken. Humanity cannot find its way without the guidance of the feminine principle. We have forgotten who we are; we no longer feel alive. Tragically, we value life less and kill more.

Old and New Paradigms of Science

The evolution of the human psyche and humankind's understanding of Self and Universe evolve together. A look at old and new paradigms of science reveals their impact upon our present world-views, and how they shape humanity's perception of the universe in which we live. Until the 1600s, the "geocentric" view of the universe prevailed; both humankind and earth were considered the center of the universe. The Copernican Revolution followed, giving birth to classical, old paradigm science, and revealing that the earth moved around the sun (heliocentric view). Classical science envisions a mechanistic, predictable, orderly cosmos and a material world of discrete, separate objects connected by a sequence of causal events.

"New" paradigm science perceives and recognizes a different universe. It is holistic, suggesting that all existence emerges from a non-material field of energy which forms and sustains Universe. Everything is interconnected and interrelated rather than discrete and separate. Earth is considered a living, aware organism; she cannot survive in fragments. In "new" paradigm science, the whole is greater than the sum of its parts.

These two scientific views seem to be polar opposites of one another. In truth, they are complementary. Each has achieved significant success in revealing the ways of nature in our world. Nevertheless, a new understanding of humanity and Universe is emerging; a radically different world-view of wholes, relationships, systems, and connections is unfolding. A more holistic world-view will be of tremendous assistance in humankind's efforts to heal Self, family, nation, and planet.

TABLE 1   Evolution of Old and New Paradigms

The Great Mother/Goddess: **"First Paradigm"**

Symbiosis–Fusion
Oceanic Unity–Oneness
Unified Psyche
Obedience to Authority
Passive
Dependent–Vulnerable
Prepersonal/Pre-egoic
Protection, Sustenance, and Nurturance
Harmony
Sacred Time and Cycles

The Patriarch   **"Old Paradigm"**

Separation, Individual, "I vs. Thou"
Either/Or, Black/White Thinking
Independence, Autonomy
Power, Control, and Domination
Deterministic, Predictable
Materialization
Technology and Specialization
Rational, Logical, Reality (Logos)
Linear Time Flow–Cause and Effect
Personal–Ego Consciousness/Shadow
Free Will–Choice
Responsible/Irresponsible
Multi-faceted

The Emerging Feminine   **"New Paradigm"**

Receptive, Intuitive (Eros)
Free Will—Choice
Responsible/Accountable
Partnership–Relational–Reconciliation
Inner Empowerment
Commitment
Interdependence/"I vs. Thou" also become "We and Us"

Interconnected/Interrelated/Wholes
Spiritual Awakening
Gateway to Transpersonal—Trans-egoic
Simultaneous Time
Both/And Thinking
Uncertainty, Unpredictability
Evolving, Emergent
Harmonious
Honors and Respects Diversity/Duality
Multi-leveled

Sacred Marriage   **"Future Paradigm"**
Union
Harmony and Balance
Commitment, Intimacy
Whole
Mind, Body, and Spirit
Non-Dual, Inclusive
Sacred Time
Co-Creator and Partnership
Spiritual Insight
Compassion
Service—Global
Multi-Dimensional
Interdependence
Diversity within Unity
Direct Experience with Numinous
Transcendental
ONE

Each organizing principle imparts a particular perception and understanding of Self, world, universe, and reality. Each world-view also determines our understanding of the arts, education, government, humanities, philosophy, psychology, the sciences, and spirituality. The Evolution of Psyche proceeds from pre-personal to personal to transpersonal/collective levels and culminates in transcendental awareness.

TRANSFORMATION

THE PROCESS

Understanding how consciousness responds whenever an individual contemplates change allows one to more fully participate in this process. The path to individuation, transformation, and wholeness, whether it is self-taught or assisted by spiritual traditions, psychological therapies, friends, or family, requires stillness and a re-examination of values and priorities.

All change involves risk; one never knows, with any certainty, what will follow. An enormous amount of trust and respect for the wisdom of the SELF is required. The process of transformation asks us to give up control and Let Go! Simple? Absolutely Not! No matter how many successes, and no matter how many times we let go... the process must be repeated, each time, anew. Hence, every change involves both a risk and a promise of personal growth.

Initially, the process of personal growth and evolution calls for quiet contemplation and focus upon needed or desired change. One begins by simply listening to Psyche. An agreement with our Self—that whatever emerges is exactly what we need to hear—is of great assistance. Never force a feeling, idea, or solution. Passively pay attention and acknowledge the contents of your mind, without judgment or censorship. Simply observe each thought and each feeling, and allow them to flow freely— in whatever direction they wish. Permit each to carry you, effortlessly, to the next.

Expect resistances—they indicate that the process is working! Our resistances often guide us to the very heart of a problem, and reveal where and how we need to grow.

Gradually permit an area of change to define itself. Allow it to evolve and to take shape. Notice how it feels to encourage its expression. Are there any feelings or attitudes that prevent you from moving toward this goal? What are the risks, challenges, and consequences of evolving in this manner? Play with your feelings and ideas. Stretch and expand them; test them out. They are your ideas; you need not be afraid of them.

The process of transformation and change takes time... days, weeks, months. Do not attempt to hurry it. Allow your Self to proceed at a comfortable pace. Remember to give your Self hugs and encouragement along the way. When you feel especially stuck, and resistances are at an all time high, give your Self well-deserved compassion and appreciation for your efforts. No one said it would be easy! Let go of where you should be, and accept where you are in the process. Recognize that transformation continues throughout your lifetime; it is an ongoing process. You are in charge. Take a risk. Take responsibility for your own life. Dare to Grow!

THE YIN AND YANG OF PERCEPTION

To embrace the wisdom of the mystic, we must suspend our rational way of understanding, and instead adopt a more intuitive, receptive mode of perception. Intellectualization and thinking actually impede our exploration of inner dimensions. To engage these levels, we must leave behind our present beliefs, attitudes, and ideas, and shift into a different perceptual mode and state of consciousness. Shifting from analytic to receptive modes offers us the possibility of beholding the wondrous ground beneath all existence. We seek to encounter SPIRIT directly and gradually to attune ourselves to see, hear, touch, and recognize the Divine in everything we do. Our direct encounters with the Numinous always impart a felt sense and experience of expanded awareness.

There are two principal modes of perception, each bestowing a different view of reality. One is rational and analytic; the other is intuitive and receptive. The first allows us to survive in the physical world; the second connects us to SOURCE and helps us explore the Path of the Heart. These seemingly opposite modes of seeing, understanding, and relating represent a fundamental cosmic duality and symbolize different stages in the evolution of Psyche. Yin (feminine and passive) and Yang (masculine and active) represent the negative and positive duality within all existence. Cosmic order reflects the ever-shifting balance between the two principles.

The first mode of rational, objective reality, is understood through measurement, analysis, reasoning, and logic. The second perceptual mode is receptive and intuitive. It honors relationship, cooperation, and harmony, and recognizes the unity of existence. Contemplation, introspection, and renunciation help guide consciousness to mysterious realms hidden from ordinary view. A still mind and an open heart are necessary for Intuitive Self to hear inspirational whisperings of SPIRIT. SPIRIT speaks to us in myths, stories, dreams, and nature. It coaxes us through music, art, poetry, waterfalls, starry nights, and ocean beaches. All are doorways to the Numinous.

TABLE 2   The Bi-Modal Structure of Consciousness

Receptive Mode	Active Mode
Receptive openness	Active engagement
Ego yields to experience	Ego centered in itself
Infusion, absorption, merger, fusion	Ego autonomy, self-possession, independence[6]

5-D Stereogram

5-D stereograms create the illusion of multidimensional images.[7] Dr. Stephen Schutz, artist and physicist, provides an example of two images within one. By a slight shift in focus, the hidden image embedded within the color matrix of the first, becomes visible.

Directions: Hold the illustration close to your nose until it becomes blurry. Stare at it, as you slowly move the picture away from your face until an image "pops out" and becomes perfectly clear. It will take practice before you begin to see the second image, so do not become discouraged. If you experience any discomfort or fatigue, stop and try again at a later time.

FIGURE 2   A 5-D Stereogram

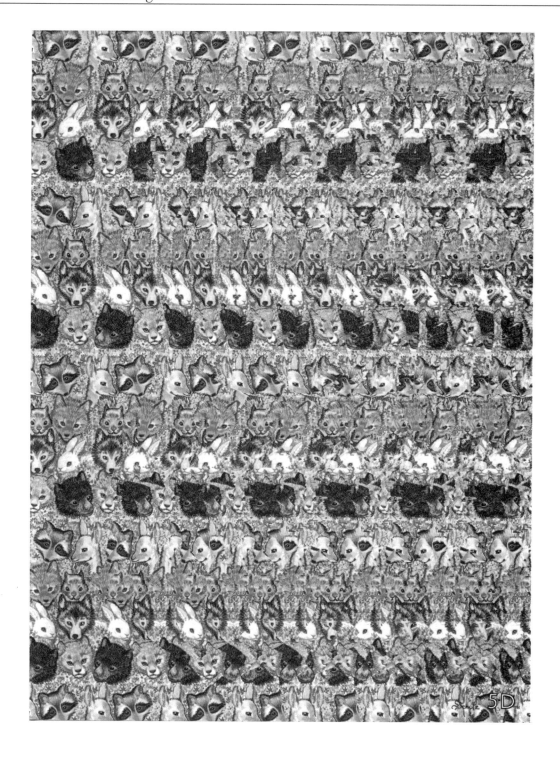

A shift from your ordinary way of seeing the world enables you to perceive another image hidden within the first. This second image reveals a row of paper dolls encircling earth.

OPTICAL ILLUSIONS

A Shift in Perception

Illusions A, B, and C contain two different images, one enfolded within the other. A slight shift in focus allows you to move between the two. What you will see depends upon your perception of figure and ground. For example, Illusion B reveals a vase if you see the dark area as the figure. If, instead, you consider this area to be the ground, the faces of two women appear. A shift in focus unfolds a different world and sense of Self. You may perceive reality through cognition and logic, or you may open to a receptive mode of viewing our world. And, if you choose, you can also realize a blending of Yin and Yang, and all the shades of gray that lie between these two polarities. Through a subtle change of intentionality and focus, Consciousness explores infinite, invisible dimensions of reality beyond the world of daily existence.

FIGURE 3   Optical Illusions

a. Rabbit or duck?

b. Vase or two women?

c. Triangle or star?

GOALS FOR THE SELF

"…there is no cure and no improving of the world that does not begin with the individual himself"[9]

The very first goal is to prioritize and arrange your life to make room for change and for the journey to unfold. It all begins with you. What is important to you? What do you really want to achieve, and what do you really believe about yourself, humanity, and your potential? Do you want to change and grow? Do you believe that you deserve good things, or instead, do you feel unworthy and inadequate?* Are you willing to confront your projections and reclaim your split-off Selves? Are you willing to become a dreamer and a visionary, as well as to share your creative yearnings and wisdom with others?

You need to determine the form of your journey and choose someone to assist and guide you along the way. The kind of journey and wholeness to which I refer requires a lifetime commitment. It cannot be gained in 3.8 sessions with a psychologist or a few months of a spiritual practice. Once you embrace this journey, it will become a lifelong part of your reality.

Your journey may begin at home, at work, or at school, in a fox-hole or a prison cell. All that matters to SOUL and Psyche† is that you make the decision to begin. Evaluate your strengths and weaknesses, and decide if you are a beginner or have already accomplished a fair amount of traveling. Your level of expertise will help determine your priorities and goals. For some, a preliminary goal to stop drinking or abusing drugs must be accomplished before embarking upon a spiritual path. For some, it means to open to the fellowship of others, or to embrace a more fulfilling way of life. For others, the journey is a response to an overwhelming urge originating from the very depths of SELF,

---

*We will deal with feelings of inadequacy and helplessness in other sections. For now, it is enough to acknowledge and honor these feelings.

†Soul is the eternal, timeless core of our Being, whereas Psyche is the essence of Consciousness which mediates between Self and Soul.

leaving very little choice but to heed its call. Each of us returns to the sacred circle on his or her own grade and level of readiness and understanding.

A worthy goal is to choose to "Be the best Self you can be," at any particular moment. It is possible to stop blaming others for the events that you do or do not experience. See what happens when you suspend criticism and judgment.

MULTI-FACETED, PERSONAL UNCONSCIOUS

Aspects and portions of our individual personhood that do not conform to the expectations and norms of parents, teachers, and society are often repressed and banished from ordinary consciousness. Our task is to reclaim these cast-off, disowned sub-personalities, inner voices, life scripts, inner children, and authentic Selves. As we personalize portions of our multi-faceted inner family (critic, saboteur, executive, defiant child, risk-taker, dreamer, and magical Self) we give them voice and meaning. Inner children represent the hopes, aspirations, fears, worries, and emotional needs a child perceives as unacceptable. These hidden, repressed, and disavowed aspects of personhood reside deep within the *personal unconscious*. Collectively, they form Psyche's shadow.

Each inner child is different; no two are alike. The vignettes below give you a flavor of different inner children and offer suggestions for contacting each. Ways to befriend and to heal your inner child vary from person to person. Experiment with different ideas and approaches until you find one that works for you.

"People Who Never Begin or End"

Many people dream about the things they want to do... someday. They plan and plan, yet never quite begin. When people believe they are "not good enough," the mere thought of starting a project gives rise to intense waves of anxiety. By "not doing," anxiety is quelled and Ego soothed. Less anxiety and discomfort are their rewards; an endless cycle of procrastination and inactivity has begun. Creativity now dwells in Psyche's shadow; Self-expression is momentarily suppressed.

Michael, your creative inner child, still wishing to explore new ideas and challenges, invites you to face your fear. He encourages you to take three deep breaths; notice your anxiety subside and calmness return. Michael wants you to know that the simple act of stilling your mind and slowing your breathing allows you to move toward your goal.

Ulla begins all her projects with ease. But Ulla always defeats herself by choosing a goal that is too big, or too difficult. Eventually, Ulla's enthusiasm will decline and her motivation fail. An overwhelmed Ulla allows the creative process to come to a screeching halt; an endless cycle of remorse and incomplete projects ensues.

Teach Ulla that it is better to divide a large project into smaller components or "baby steps." Every completed step grants its own reward; step by step, Ulla attains her goal. She is filled with awe, wonder, and pride; she feels ten feet tall.

Recognizing the ways your inner child sabotages your hopes and dreams lets you design new strategies to reach your goals. Expressing your creativity and uniqueness allows a Universe to unfold.

Richard—The Bashful Child

Richard is a shy child, especially adept at being unobtrusive and silent. He is afraid of making contact with others; being with other people is unbearable. He never knows what to say. "Careful Richard, don't smile or call attention to yourself! Wheww - that was close." If only someone, anyone, would speak and draw attention away from me. "Whew! Thanks. That's better. Now I can breathe again."

How do you make contact with a painfully shy inner child who prefers not to meet you? Sit quietly beside Richard; let him sense your presence. Do not hurry him. Reassure Richard that you are his friend. Let him know it is alright to be silent; tell him how much you value this special quality.

As Richard becomes more trusting, you might tell him how much you enjoy being with him. Invite him to share his loneliness and end his isolation. As you open your heart and listen, Richard will appear more frequently; each time he will remain a bit longer. Let him know how important he is to you. Your patience will help Richard grow in confidence. In time, you may even learn why Richard retreated into shyness. Perhaps he'll come to trust you enough to tell you that he wants you to visit with him more often. Allow plenty of time to befriend your bashful child. Your efforts will allow Richard to heal and grow and in return, he will bring you joy and serenity.

Susan—A Sexually Abused Child

Susan has a haunted, frightened look on her pretty face. She is always vigilant, always on guard, never able to relax or be still. Although Susan pleases and acquieses to the demands of others, she finds no peace. Rage, anger, and desperation, along with an ever present sense of powerlessness, stir within her.

Today, Susan is especially tense and vigilant. She knows that she will be invited to bed by her step-dad, and that it is futile to protest. She catches a glimpse of her mother in the living room. As her mother turns away, Susan recognizes the fear in her mother's eyes. Susan knows her mother will do nothing to intercede. Feelings of anger and betrayal overwhelm Susan. The door closes behind her and she is alone with her step-dad. Disrobing, she silently climbs into bed. She feels the warm breath of her step-dad upon her. ... At last, he leaves her alone.

It is quiet. Susan is alone with her thoughts and feelings. She knows them well. Shame and anguish rush in and there is a sense of violation. As tears stream down her face, she shoves her rage aside. Waves of anguish and despair wash over Susan. Denial and repression sweep in to protect her. Slowly and with great pain and effort, Susan climbs out of bed and bathes herself. Eight-year-old Susan feels old and tired. Finally, she crawls back to bed and falls asleep.

As Susan matures, she will feel confused, empty, and disturbed. She will not understand why she feels as she does, for she has banished her "secret" shame to Psyche's shadow. Susan is unable to confront its full terror. The more severe and enduring the abuse, the greater is the need for denial.

Although outwardly provocative, Susan avoids sexual intimacy and disappoints the men she unconsciously tempts. Susan will act out her rage and hate against men, in ever more destructive cycles, unconsciously seeking their betrayal so that she can re-experience shame and guilt. Essentially, Susan provokes the men in her life to re-enact the sexual drama of abuse, humiliation, and victimization she experienced at an earlier age. Her despair and pain will escalate.

How can you help Susan face the ugly secret she hides? Can you teach her that her pattern of secrecy, avoidance, and self-destruction only prolongs her pain and humiliation? Start by acknowledging her wish to escape and to hide. Share compassion, not pity, with Susan. A sense of trust must be in place before Susan can share her secret(s) with you. You will need lots of patience and time. Do not hurry Susan.

Gradually... slowly... Susan will allow her painful memories to come to the surface and tell their story. Once she shares her secret with you, she will find herself experiencing feelings of guilt and betrayal for having done so. At this special moment, she will be engulfed in shame and pain, and more vulnerable than ever before! Hold her, nurture her, and reassure her that she is good and kind. This is an important moment to be with Susan.

Listen to Susan's anger and memories. Encourage her to relive the experience as often as she needs to. Let her know that sexual abuse is never the child's fault; relieve Susan of this heavy responsibility. The bruises and scars of sexual abuse run deep. Psychotherapy and emotional support can help both Susan and you to heal. As shame recedes, Susan will seek love in healthier ways.

The four inner children above need compassion, empathy, and patience in order to heal and to trust again. It takes a lot of time and encouragement to work through pain, to risk, and to love. Healing and integrating the split-off, dissociated portions of personal Selfhood makes us whole. As we become more whole, a fuller humanity emerges and we touch the divine.

Conversations with your inner Self enable your fullest potential to unfold. New goals might include being kind, loving, compassionate, available, honest, attentive, dependable, patient, liking yourself better, and forgiving.

DIALOGUE WITH A PRESENT SELF

Determining the Growth and Changes You Desire

You may wish to record this visualization into a tape recorder, or ask a friend to guide you through it. Allow approximately 20-25 minutes to complete this exercise.

Close your eyes and find a comfortable position. Visualize your Self resting in a favorite place, a place where you can simply be and relax. Know you are safe in this space!

Take three or four deep breaths at your own pace and feel your body and mind begin to slow down and relax. Continue to breathe slowly and rhythmically as you become aware of your chest moving up and down with each breath.

Feel a sense of relaxation move from your toes and heels, up your calves, and into your knees. Let relaxation flow from your knees to your thighs, and into your pelvis, hips, and lower back.

Feel tension slip away from your body. Allow this sense of relaxation and well-being to move into your chest, your upper back, and your shoulders. Feel it gently slide down your arms—all the way to your elbows, right down to your fingertips.

Sense calmness spreading through your neck, over your scalp, onto your face, and back, again, to your neck and torso.

You are now enfolded in a cocoon of healing energy. Perhaps your arms and legs are beginning to feel limp and heavy. You may even feel tingling or warmth throughout your entire body. These are normal sensations indicating that you are deeply relaxed.

1/2 minute of silence—just experience this state of calmness.

You are ready to visit with your Present Self. The purpose of this meditation is to discover the ways and the areas in which you might grow and discover your potential as a whole human being. Remember, you are in control. You can discontinue this exercise anytime that you wish.

We experience many deaths and rebirths throughout our lives, not just during childhood. Hence, we are continually creating and repressing certain aspects of our Selves that wish to be expressed. Why do we deny our own individuality and personhood? What purpose can there be in "holding your Self" back and avoiding your dreams? Take a minute or so to ponder this question and examine the feelings that arise.

Acknowledge whatever you experience. 1 minute of silence.

Most of us have areas of dissatisfaction in our lives. We often consider making changes or expanding our visions, only to collapse into a space of stuckness. Some of us wish to move to a different city or state. Others wish to return to a simpler style of life or move into retirement. Many are seeking new jobs that require new skills. Some feel trapped in relationships that are no longer growing. Others feel terribly alone and are searching for new relationships, intimacy, and commitment. Some parents want to see their children grow up and move out on their own, while other couples are just opening to the promise and fulfillment of parenthood. Many of us are ready to leave our sense of victimhood behind and to assume greater responsibility for our lives.

Take a few moments to consider your own PRESENT. Where are you in your LIFE? What do you like and what do you want to change?

1 minute silence.

As you consider your Present state, listen to the thoughts and ideas that run through your psyche. Are they thoughts that are helpful, or ones that will hold you back? What are the feelings and sensations which accompany your thoughts?

1 minute silence.

Take a moment to tune in to your body. Is it tense or relaxed? Simply notice places of tension and tightness in your body. As your awareness shifts to your body, notice how tension gently eases into relaxation, and breathing automatically slows.

I minute silence.

How can you change and grow in your Present life? The first step is to become aware of what you wish to transform.

Examine and define some areas in need of change. Next, become aware of your feelings, ideas, and thoughts. Simply become aware and allow your feelings and thoughts to emerge into consciousness. Pay attention to feelings of resistance and stuckness, as well as acknowledge your dreams, hopes, and desires. Appreciate that any stuckness and resistance to change keeps you SAFE. It is one solution. However, growth and evolution are other choices.

Listen to your Self, and determine your willingness and readiness to grow and to move forward. Do you feel resistance and fear—or joy and excitement? Acknowledge whatever feeling or thought arises; it is exactly what you need to experience at this time. Your resistances reveal most accurately where and how you might change.

2 minutes silence.

Dialogue with your Present Self. Experience the longing and yearning for transformation and creativity that the Present Self desires.

1 1/2 minutes silence.

How do you feel now that you have defined an area of transformation and growth? Are you experiencing fear and anxiety, or are you excited about moving into this newer reality? Let your Present Self know if you are willing and ready to support its need and desire for transformation. If you are not prepared to change at this time, share this with your Present Self.

1 minute silence.

Consider the request for change and growth that your Present Self has made. Are you willing to actualize and move toward your dreams? Feel the sense of empowerment that accompanies a decision to grow.

1 minute silence.

Tell your Present Self that you were glad to meet him or her. If you wish, the two of you can arrange a date and time for your next visit. Remember, don't make any promises you cannot keep!

1 minute.

Now bid your Present Self goodbye! Sense how it feels to say farewell. Are you numb, sad, relieved, elated, or indifferent? Watch your inner Self fade into the distance, and gently return your attention to an awareness of your breath, and your body. Gradually return your focus back to this room and to the sounds that surround you. Begin to count from 1 to 5. At the count of 5, open your eyes and feel relaxed and refreshed.

1...   2...   3...   4...   5...

Before you share your encounters with your Present Self, use the stenciled doll mandala included with this visualization. Using colors, symbols, words, or whatever you choose, non-verbally express your impressions of your visit. This stenciled doll will serve as a mandala of today's journey. You may wish to write a few sentences and thoughts in a journal. If you find that you were unable to define an area of change, or that you are not quite ready to follow through on a particular path of transformation, you might express this realization.

SELF

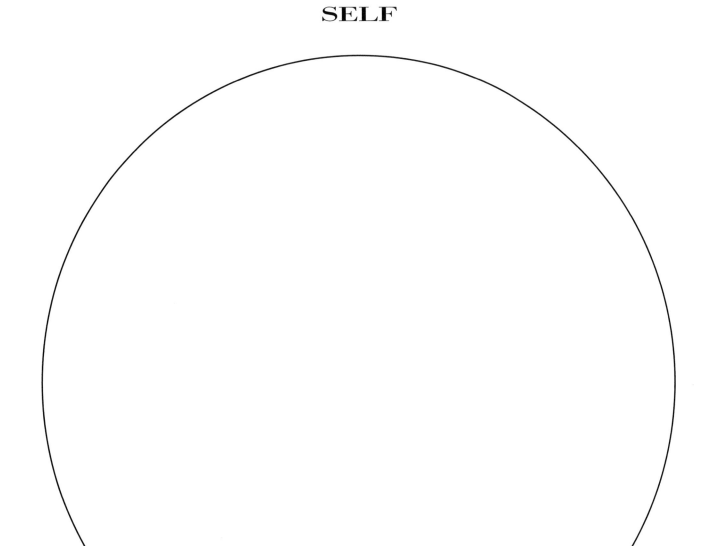

MULTI-LEVELED, COLLECTIVE UNCONSCIOUS

While inner children and split-off, repressed elements echo the personal issues and experiences of each individual, archetypes paint a broader canvas. Emerging from the depths of Psyche, archetypes belong to the whole of humanity irrespective of race, religion, nationality, or year of birth.*

Archetypes

Archetypes psychically influence and program our individual choices, personal goals, and struggles throughout life. Various archetypal elements come into play at different stages of Psyche's evolution and development. In *Once Upon ASOUL,* I define them as Great Mother/Goddess, Patriarch/Masculine, and the Feminine. Jungian analyst Carol Pearson[10] also describes a predictable sequence of human development governed by six different archetypes she identifies as Innocent, Orphan, Wanderer, Warrior, Martyr, and Magician. Pearson tells us that Innocent lives in a perpetual state of bliss, grace, and trust, whereas Orphan must confront the harsh Fall from Paradise and the task of caring for its own needs. Orphan, desiring security and safety above all else, frequently acquiesces to the wishes of others. No wonder Orphan perpetually feels betrayed, exploited, and abandoned. Wanderer, challenged to define a separate and independent personhood, avoids conformity, seeks autonomy, and sets forth to establish a brave new world. Martyr is self-sacrificing, self-effacing, and embroiled in the eternal struggle between good and evil. Martyr must learn to sacrifice for others without sacrificing Self. Warrior strives to be strong and in control of people and situations. Warrior's challenge is to discover an inner strength, recognize the interconnectivity and interrelationship of all existence, and to cooperatively work with others. The hero/heroine who embraces the holy grail within, is transformed into the Magician. Magician bestows deepened awareness, self-trust, and harmony with all existence. The path of the hero/heroine travels from victimhood, to self-definition, to empowerment, to wholeness. When Magician uncovers an inner paradise and wisdom, the journey is complete.†

Once Upon ASOUL, Section 4, provides more information on Archetypes.

†You may recognize that Innocent represents Communion and the blessings of life under the Great Mother. Orphan recapitulates the "Slaying of the Dragon" and the Fall from Paradise. Wanderer, Martyr, and Warrior all dwell under the rule of the Patriarch and seek independence and separation. Magician completes the circle and learns to live with paradox and duality. Magician successfully unites Feminine and Masculine and attains wholeness and serenity. For a more comprehensive discussion of these ideas, refer to *Once Upon ASOUL*.

Each archetypal organizing principle filters and colors Psyche's perception of personhood, family, society, and world in its own unique way, weaving and influencing the multitudinous levels and dimensions of existence. For example, if we arbitrarily assign the color yellow to Matriarchal consciousness, Psyche will perceive its world primarily through this yellow lens. Men, women, family, society, science, psychology, and spirituality appear sunshiney yellow. Communion, First Peoples, the innocence of Childhood, and pre-Egoic consciousness come only in yellow. But Patriarchal consciousness is blue in hue. Hence, Separation, Individuation, Ego-consciousness, adolescence, and the quest for autonomy can only be found in shades of blue. By endowing Feminine consciousness with rose-pink overtones, Psyche engages a rose-colored world of relationship, healing, redemption, and Ex-centric awareness. And union and reconciliation of Masculine and Feminine paint Psyche's world with lavender flavors, as blue and pink tones blend into sacred marriage and a lilac world-view. Essentially, each principle reflects and defines the individual and collective understanding and perceptions of a particular age. What you see is up to you; your world-view and perception will faithfully echo your level of awareness and consciousness. Some of us presently live in a yellow world, others dwell in a world of blue. Still others seek to experience a rosey-pink domain which will serve as a gateway to a transcendent lavender universe. Regardless of hue or name, each world has its own unique look, feel, smell, taste, and possibilities. Which world do you live in? Which world do you aspire to? It is truly up to you.

PORTRAIT OF A MARTYR—MARILYN AND RAY

The Martyr archetype brings to mind my clients, Marilyn and Ray, who were planning his company's annual gathering. Previous parties had been fun, but they had also involved organization and work, especially on Marilyn's part. This particular year, Marilyn was eager to please Ray and she immersed herself in planning the event. The day of the party arrived and everything seemed to proceed effortlessly. Yet, a tearful Marilyn felt a growing resentment. Realizing that she did not have enough people to assist with clean-up and dishes, she stoically rescued the party. Marilyn donned an apron and unhesitantly took charge. The party was a success, but Marilyn was exhausted. When all the guests had departed, Ray turned around to thank Marilyn. She never heard what he had to say, because she was consumed with hurt, resentment, and anger. How could he have allowed her be a maid at the firm party? How could he have taken advantage of her willingness to help? The party was expensive, very expensive. Why hadn't anyone arranged for a clean-up crew? Marilyn ranted and complained, while

Ray looked at the ceiling. He recognized that her need for help was legitimate and felt ashamed that he had never encouraged his wife to get more assistance. He assumed she would take care of it. Although they had hosted a wonderful party for one and all, both went to sleep depleted and angry.

The next morning, with my help, Marilyn began to take back the anger and blame she had projected upon Ray. She began to suspect that she had failed her Self. She had not considered her own needs and limitations, nor had she admitted her desire to be a guest at her own party. She had expected someone out there to take care of her. When help did not come, she had blamed Ray. Gradually, she began to recognize her own reluctance to ask for help. She made a commitment to begin nurturing her Self by setting firm limits on what she would and would not do at the next party. She was beginning to honor her Self and no longer needed to be a Martyr or to project blame upon Ray. The next year's party was not only a success, it was a pleasant experience for Marilyn. Ray was also delighted to have his wife by his side rather than in the kitchen. Marilyn's willingness to confront her projections opened the door to more positive solutions. Perhaps, like Marilyn, you have difficulty asking for help or consideration. What do you do when you fail to get your needs acknowledged?

CARLOS—THE ANONYMOUS BENEFACTOR

Carlos adored helping people; it was his calling. He never felt compelled or obligated to help others; he simply felt better whenever he did. One afternoon, he came to see me. He was concerned about his friend who had recently lost his job and was unable to buy Christmas gifts for his children. It reminded Carlos of his first Christmas in the orphanage; he was only 7 years old. How he missed his mother and his sister! Wouldn't it be wonderful if they would come to see him. Maybe, just maybe, they would surprise him with a toy or a piece of candy. The hours ticked by, and Carlos slowly realized they were not coming. In his loneliness and desolation, Carlos made a vow that he would never stand by and watch another child spend Christmas alone.

Carlos remembered his promise and decided to help his friend; he placed two $20.00 bills into an unmarked envelope. It was his last $40.00. Carlos left the money in his friend's mailbox on his way home. The money would buy dinner and toys for this family. His friends would have a real Christmas.

Carlos' astonished friends found the money later that day. They rushed to the store to purchase gifts for the children and food for Christmas dinner. They felt truly blessed. His friends never did learn the identity of their mysterious benefactor. Carlos was not interested in thank-you's, recognition, or gratitude; he purposely left no name or address on the envelope. Carlos' was a simple act of loving kindness; it filled his Soul with a warm glow.

Acts of loving kindness seem to help those who give as well as those who receive. Recent research suggests that service to others can enhance your own well-being. A Michigan study of 2,700 men found that community volunteers had a longer life span than peers who did not make serving others an integral part of their lives. This is the real meaning of the biblical phrase, "To give is to receive."

HEALING THE MIND-BODY CENTER

Another beneficial goal is to get back into your own body. All too often we live only above our necks, intellectualizing and analyzing our behavior while avoiding any feelings or sensations that could tell us what we really feel and know deep inside of our Selves. Allow your Self to have an "In-Body" experience.

Rose

Rose is a woman who lived in her head, totally unable to experience any kind of pain or emotion. The first time I met Rose, she was in the midst of chemotherapy for breast cancer. It was the second time that cancer had been diagnosed. She came to see me because her doctor had sent her; he thought she had an "attitude problem" and believed that I might help her. The first thing I noticed was her monotone voice and the blank expression on her face as she recited her medical history and related a life of constant physical abuse. She informed me that she was a survivor and she would recover. "No need to worry, it was no big deal." She proudly let me know that she didn't need any help; she was strong. Her denial and defiance reverberated through me. She had imprisoned her Self behind walls of hurt and rage so that no one would know how scared and frightened she really was.

Over time, Rose gradually allowed me to enter her world. She began to trust me and to share her pain, both psychological and physical. She started to deal with the helpless rage she had turned against her body because she did not know how to externalize it. Her cancer was spreading all too quickly, despite medical efforts. Months later, Rose realized that the cancer was stronger than she. She collapsed into despair and depression. We formed a partnership and, together, we confronted her approaching death. It was an intense time for both of us.

Courageously, Rose learned to stay in her body and to allow her feelings and pain. She discovered a softer, more gentle strength and confidence in her last few days. I miss her still.

As we develop our body awareness, we often become unwilling to eat foods that do not nourish us, such as junk foods and fast foods. We will probably want to exercise and move our bodies to keep them physically fit and limber. We will no longer want to work 70-80 hours per week when we come "alive" inside our skin. Instead, we may choose to slow down when we are tired, and follow the rhythms and cycles of work, nourishment, play, and rest that our bodies require in order to keep us healthy, active, and functional.

For those who wish to do the work of integrating shadow and light, of healing the split between inner and outer worlds, and of uniting the masculine and feminine forces of Psyche, the ultimate goal is one of balance, harmony, and wholeness through self-realization. The goals of the Self can span all the levels of Selfhood: personal, existential, collective unconscious, transpersonal, transcendental, and beyond.

TECHNIQUES AND METHODS

Some techniques are immediate and quite simple. Others require more discipline, preparation, and commitment. We will start with the simplest and move to more involved possibilities. I offer only a few ideas and suggestions, since real change and growth come through the felt experience and by doing, not by thinking, talking, or reading about it. Change and transform are verbs, reminding us we are always in the process of unfolding.

RE-INVENTING THE SABBATH

A Sabbath is a sacred space for rest and reflection. It affords a respite from the pressures and activities of the physical world. A weekly Sabbath would occasion the healing of our bodies and minds, and afford us time for inner communion with ASOUL. Refreshed and spiritually nourished, we return to the world of the senses, feeling more whole and peaceful at the end of an hour or a day of At-One-Ment.

Light a candle and invite a friend to light one too. Join your candles and experience the larger light the two of you, together, bring into the world.

ADOPTION

Adopt a whale or a dolphin. Without protective action, many large sea mammals face mass extinction.

Dolphin Encounter

On the last day of my Hawaiian vacation, I had an opportunity to play with two bottlenose dolphins. Two dolphins swam toward me, as I timidly entered the lagoon. I was introduced to Pelé, a 300 pound female and Lono, a 400 pound male. Their trainer invited me to gently stroke Pelé's body; her skin felt soft, smooth, and had a "vinyl" feel. Pelé joyfully rolled over and over, to let me know how much she enjoyed being stroked.

For a magical half hour, I swam and played with Pelé and Lono. They entertained me with their many tricks, asking only to be stroked in exchange. Their trainer continually asked me to cheer, praise, and love these water babies. I wondered what would happen if I openly and unashamedly lavished the same kind of praise upon my family and friends. I was certain that human beings would respond as favorably to praise and caring.

All too soon, my encounter with Pelé and Lono came to an end. I bid each good-bye and left the lagoon, refreshed and pleased. Dolphins are loving, gentle, and adorable; each dolphin is a "volunteer." They urgently need humankind's help in keeping the seas and oceans safe, if they are to survive.[*] Whatever you do to assist dolphin survival, you do as well for planetary survival. Please help all you can to make earth a safe dwelling place for one and all.

Human beings are also an endangered species; children require the nurturing assistance of Mothering Ones. Throughout the world, needy and impoverished children await our rescue. A deeply satisfying sense of helping can be yours when you adopt a foster child or feed the hungry and poor.

---

[*]Please buy chicken, turkey, and "dolphin-free tuna," use low phosphate detergents, and cut plastic rings around 6 and 12-packs of soda and beer. Plastic rings have proven dangerous, even deadly, to these benevolent beings.

CREATIVE ENDEAVORS

Poetry, drama, art, and sculpture, as well as dance, drumming, and music possess healing properties. They communicate non-verbally to Psyche on many levels. The arts encourage us at times of stuckness and pain, as well as multiply the depth and richness of our joy. The themes and rhythms of the arts enhance our journeys and often "set the stage" for altered states of consciousness, growth, and transformation. Creativity is food and nourishment for SOUL.

Food for the Soul

Whenever I crave Soul food, I do some of the following: I walk in the woods, hug a grandchild, play the flute, share a romantic dinner with my husband, bake bread, smell a rose, or look at the star-studded heavens. And I try to do things that make me laugh. Laughter lightens my heart and gladdens my Soul. Joy allows me to touch my humanity and sense the wonder and mystery of life.

When I crave time and communion with my Soul, I meditate, I sit under a tree, arrange flowers, needlepoint, or just stay still. In a space of silence, I often hear the voice of Spirit shift my thoughts to more life-sustaining ideas and action. Guided and blessed, I return to the world of everyday life refreshed and energized.

Sometimes my Soul cries out for companionship, yearning for comaraderie with others who can nourish my psyche and/or heal my pain. There are times when I do not wish to be alone and seek out those who will give me comfort and love. I reach out to my friends by telephone and Internet — "Are you there?" Sometimes, when no one is home, I turn to my dog and cat. They are wonderful friends and companions.

What do you do to refresh your Soul? Are you so busy doing, that you have forgotten how to be? Are you suffering from "hurry-up" sickness and endlessly filling your days consuming, doing, and buying? How long is it since you smelled the flowers, walked on the beach, or took a day off to be with your lover and/or children?

Do you know that you have a Soul? Have you ever spoken to the inner core of your Self and listened to its response? Reach out to Soul, and recognize that you are never alone. Sit quietly and discover the One You Are; you will be glad that you did.

ACTIVITIES TO ASSIST MOTHER EARTH

Consider hugging and rescuing a tree. You will feel a greater sense of connection with nature and the cosmos. Feed ducks, recycle cans and paper, create a garden, and know that you are assisting the planet and replenishing earth's resources.

Papa Flower Blossom

Gardens always remind me of David. David spent a lot of time and energy repressing his feelings and thoughts, and was only dimly aware of the pain, hurt, and fear that lurked within his heart. He was always tired and wondered why. Keeping a lid on his rage left him very little energy for joy.

Some weeks after David started psychotherapy, he decided to start a rose garden. Timidly (a feeling), he planted several rose bushes. He gradually learned about organic and pesticide-free gardening, and how to prepare his own mulch. He studied everything he could about roses. David's flowers responded to his love and passion (more feelings). They bloomed profusely, and David experienced a sense of pride. He began to enjoy his time outdoors and his new found partnership with nature. Gardening took David out of his head and back into his body, enabling him to touch his pain and acknowledge his anger. He learned ways to deal with his emotions, providing space for more positive sensations and experience. As David healed and nurtured his plants, he healed and nurtured his own psyche. His family proudly referred to him as "Papa Flower Blossom." Assisting Mother Earth is one of the most beneficial things we can do for our Selves. What is good for our planet, is also good for us.

TRANSFORMING THE ORDINARY INTO THE EXTRAORDINARY

Eastern mystics suggest that it is in the everyday activities of life that one finds divinity. They advise us to, "Chop Wood and Carry Water." In modern terms, we can begin our spiritual pathways merely by folding laundry, washing the dishes, baking bread, cleaning the garage, walking the dog, and doing our everyday chores and jobs. Our attitude and willingness to co-create with Universe distinguishes the profane from the holy, and returns a sense of the sacred to our lives.

RELAXATION, STRESS REDUCTION, AND GUIDED IMAGERY

When new clients start psychotherapy, I teach them to breathe in and out, quietly and slowly. It is a way for them to get into their bodies and out of their heads. The body and mind both slow down, enabling us to relax and gradually pay attention to deeper processes. I teach clients a system of progressive relaxation so that they can instantly relax, even in the midst of a crisis. The following cognitive-behavioral exercise helps us become aware of our interconnection and deep relatedness to the environment.

Exercise

Walk slowly for ten minutes, choosing a pace half your normal walking speed. Observe what you see and feel throughout your stroll. It is a relaxing, simple, and most impressive exercise, one that informs both the body and the mind. You will be surprised at what happens as a consequence of stretching the moment.

Craig—Too Nervous to Relax

Craig came to see me because he was anxious and tense all the time. We decided to do some relaxation training. No one tried harder than Craig, but he couldn't seem to let go enough to enter into a state of relaxation. Craig would take three deep, rhythmic breaths, but he always stopped just before reaching a space of calmness.

After a few weeks of trying, we both decided to honor his resistance. I asked Craig what he did in times of stress and agitation. He smiled and took out his rosary beads. Suddenly, we both knew exactly what Craig needed to do in order to relax. As he moved his fingers from bead to bead, his breath slowed, his mind let go of control, and his body relaxed. Craig had discovered his own special way to relax.

Many of us can enter into a state of relaxation quickly and easily using the exercises below. Try them and see if they work for you. Feel free to modify them to your own needs.

Healing Breath

Find a quiet place and allow yourself 15-20 minutes to complete this exercise. You may sit or lie down; choose whatever position is most comfortable. Close your eyes and focus on your breathing; slowly inhale and exhale. Notice how your abdomen rises up and down with each breath you take. Breathe yourself into a place of stillness. There is nothing else you must do. Slowly allow the "Breath of the Invisible" to fill your lungs and penetrate all the tissues and cells inside your body. Feel the cool air flow from your nose, to your throat, to your trachea, and into both lungs. And when you are ready, slowly exhale the warm breath that rises deep within your lungs and let it connect you to All that surrounds you.

Repeat this cycle of inhalation and exhalation for several minutes. Become aware of a growing calmness that fills your lungs with each breath, and notice the release of tension with each exhalation. Whenever you feel ready, return your attention to your body, the room in which you are, and the sounds of the outer world. Slowly and gradually open your eyes, and notice how refreshed you feel.

Progressive Relaxation Technique

You may wish to record this exercise into a tape recorder, or ask a friend to guide you through it. Allow approximately 20 minutes to complete it.

Close your eyes and find a comfortable position. Visualize your Self resting in a favorite place, a place where you can simply be and relax. Know you are safe in this space!

Take three or four deep breaths at your own pace and feel your body and mind begin to slow down and relax. Continue to breathe slowly and rhythmically as you become aware of your chest moving up and down with each breath.

Allow a sense of relaxation to move from your toes and heels, up your calves and into your knees. Let relaxation flow from your knees to your thighs, and into your pelvis, hips, and lower back.

Feel tension slip away from your body. Allow this sense of relaxation and well-being to move into your chest, your upper back, and your shoulders. Feel it gently slide down your arms—all the way to your elbows, right down to your fingertips.

Sense calmness spreading through your neck, over your scalp, onto your face, and back, again, to your neck and torso. You are now enfolded in a cocoon of healing energy.

Your arms and legs may feel limp and heavy. You may even feel tingling or warmth throughout your entire body. These are normal sensations that accompany deep relaxation.

Take a few moments to experience this state of calmness. If you feel tense, focus your attention on this part of your body where tension exists. There is nothing else you have to do. Notice what happens when you bring your attention to a place of tightness in your body. Just acknowledging a place of tension often releases it. If you feel anxiety, focus your attention upon this spot. Again, all you have to do is acknowledge its presence, and the anxiety will fade away. Gradually, feel a sense of well-being and control return.

Whenever you wish to engage the world of the senses, gently return your attention to an awareness of your breath and your body. Gradually, shift your focus back to this room and to the sounds that surround you. Begin to count from 1 to 5. At the count of 5, open your eyes and feel relaxed and refreshed. 1... 2... 3... 4... 5...

Creating a Place of Safety

Use the Progressive Relaxation script to enter and leave a place of calmness. Between the beginning and end, add:

Think of a very special place that is safe and comfortable... a place where you can safely retreat and take care of yourself... a place to visit whenever you need to heal and replenish your body and spirit. ... I will provide an image of a special place and you may add personal details and touches to make it uniquely your own. ...

Imagine yourself in a beautiful forest. You are walking along a narrow pathway, lined with tall trees. You walk until you come to a clearing in the woods. A gentle breeze caresses the forest. Imagine that you are sitting against one of the tall, tall trees that lovingly welcomes your presence. Notice a small building or house in the clearing. This is your special sanctuary—a place of complete peace and security.

Enter through the door and notice a cozy fire burning in the fireplace. Your favorite music fills the room. As you sit down, you can hear the songs of the birds outside your window. Glance around this room and notice that all your favorite books and things surround you. If you wish, bring your favorite pet into this room with you.

Take a few minutes to arrange your shelter as you wish it to be. Choose the colors, textures, and furnishings you want to surround you. Know that you can return to this place as often as you wish. You are welcome and safe here. It is your private sanctuary.

Whenever you wish to engage the world of the senses, gently return your awareness to your breath and your body. Gradually, shift your focus back to your everyday room and to the sounds that surround you. Begin to count from 1 to 5. At the count of 5, open your eyes and feel relaxed and refreshed. 1... 2... 3... 4... 5...

You may wish to describe your sanctuary and how you have decorated it in your journal. You may also wish to write down your feelings and impressions of discovering your special hide-away.

Meeting a Wisdom Teacher

Use the Progressive Relaxation exercise to enter into a state of receptivity and relaxation. In the middle, add:

See yourself at the end of a very dense forest. Find a stone pathway that disappears into the trees. Walk down this path, feeling the stones under your feet. Perceive smells, songs of birds, and bask in the gentle, filtered light that shines through the trees. Take as much time to rest and to walk deep into the woods as you need. There is no urgency or need to hurry. As you move deeper and deeper into the lush forest, you begin to perceive a hazy light ahead. Move toward the light.

Walk into the light and into a clearing. Notice the colors, smells, and textures of this meadow. Find a place to sit. It could be a large rock, a fallen log, or just a grassy knoll. Make yourself comfortable and wait for something magical to happen.

Your visitor might be an animal, a bird, or a person. This person might even be a wise old man or woman who looks like you will, many years from now. Do not be afraid... this messenger has come in peace. Make eye to eye contact with your visitor. Reach out and touch one another. It will not hurt you.

If you have a question, ask it... and then humbly receive your answer. Hold the answer in your mind and thank your guide for coming and bringing you this treasure. Whenever you are ready, say goodbye to this special visitor.

Leave by the same pathway you came; walk back into the woods moving briskly, as you are now familiar with this path. When ready, open your eyes and return your attention to your everyday reality. Notice how refreshed and energized you feel.

It is a good idea to record your questions and answers in a journal, as well as to write down your feelings and impressions. Journal entries permit you to follow your own growth and evolution over time. If a wisdom teacher fails to visit, or you did not receive an answer to your question, write down how you feel about your experience.

Creating your own tapes and imagery scripts

It is best to learn one script at a time, to avoid confusing your psyche. Become familiar with a particular exercise before you try another one. Use the progressive relaxation technique to enter and leave any script you design. Some people prefer to record their own voices, and use their own names throughout a taped exercise. A personalized tape makes it easier to let go and trust. Music enhances your state of relaxation and your ability to visualize. Tapes may be created to stimulate healing, prepare for surgery, alter your state of consciousness, and to commune with Soul.

PSYCHOTHERAPY AND SUPPORT GROUPS

Others might prefer to heal Self and family on the physical plane. Their practice might take the form of psychotherapy. All psychotherapies initially work to heal the split between shadow and ego, and to encourage development of the deep morality and ethics necessary for exploring multidimensional levels of personhood.

What is Psychotherapy?

My clients often ask me to define the process of psychotherapy. I consider psychotherapy to be an interactive process leading to growth, insight, and change. As a psychologist, I contribute my knowledge and skills to create a safe, supportive environment in which each person can express thoughts, feelings, and needs without criticism or judgment. Clients bring a desire for help, as well as a commitment to work on important issues. The process of psychotherapy teaches individuals how to set limits, to clarify personal goals, values, and priorities and to seek new solutions to old problems. Clients learn more effective coping skills and to assume responsibility for feelings and behavior, thereby facilitating more satisfying relationships and more fulfilling, productive lives.

Brief Short-Term Psychotherapy is useful for defining issues, setting goals, resolving specific problems, and for individuals in crisis.

Long-Term Psychotherapy provides enhanced self-awareness and growth that opens to personal transformation.

Group Psychotherapy creates a social microcosm for each of the members who relate to the other members in the group in essentially the same manner that they relate to individuals in the outside world. Group process captures the patterns of feelings, thoughts, and behavior "in the act," enabling an individual to see his/her own interpersonal and intrapersonal issues clearly. Groups often provide a space for an individual to experience intimacy and acceptance for the first time.

As a psychologist, I often work with couples. Many of us are discovering that our relationships with others reveal, with great clarity, the myriad ways in which each partner needs to change. Healing of the split between shadow and ego, and the reclaiming of our projections, become the content of our couple's work. Each partner offers the other the opportunity to become whole on this level. Since process in relationships is frequently intense, it often accelerates the transformation and spiritual growth for all involved. As process continues, a couple may find that their partnership extends beyond the more limited relationship they first knew.

Humanistic and Transpersonal schools of psychology recognize that each of us continues to develop and evolve throughout our entire life span. A growing awareness and deepened consciousness are considered necessary steps toward a more mature expression of humanhood. These schools are often gateways into life's mysteries.

The process of transformation requires courage and risk. It is not enough to gain insight and to take responsibility, although these are necessary and important first steps. We must also find the motivation, the willingness, and the courage to engage Psyche on many levels, and to become more conscious co-creators of our own lives. The true efficacies of any spiritual or psychological practice are change and action. Only through awareness, responsibility, and the desire to change can we realize our dreams, visions, and destinies.

The Mandala

Recognition of a circular-spiral SELF, existing on many levels and dimensions, helps each of us overcome our present limitations and attachments; we become free to embrace ASOUL. Images of circles, mandalas, medicine wheels, and spirals often appear in dreams and visions. They symbolically proclaim Psyche's need for structure, harmony, balance, and new personhood. Mandala and medicine wheel are sacred maps to the Realms of Spirit. They tell us it is time for us to grow.

Mandalas echo the structural order in Universe; they speak of life and death, becoming and transcending. Whether one reflects and meditates upon complex religious mandalas, or spontaneously creates one from strands of dreams and reverie, mandalas remind us we are part of ALL THAT IS. In truth, every individual is a mandala; each cycle of life forever intertwined with the eternal rhythms and cycles of Universe.[11]

Since the mandala unites heaven and earth, and joins matter and non-matter, it is simultaneously personal and transpersonal. Mandalas release unconscious energies and creativity into consciousness, express both dark and light sides of Psyche, and inform us of new directions and possibilities.

I encourage you to paint a mandala once a week for at least a month. A series of mandala images will accurately reveal changes in your personal understanding, perception, and development. Notice how colors, patterns, and themes are transformed as your insight grows and matures. All forms and colors flow outwardly from the center toward the periphery of your image. The center is nameless and eternal, a place of self-renewal and rebirth. The center is every Self's goal.

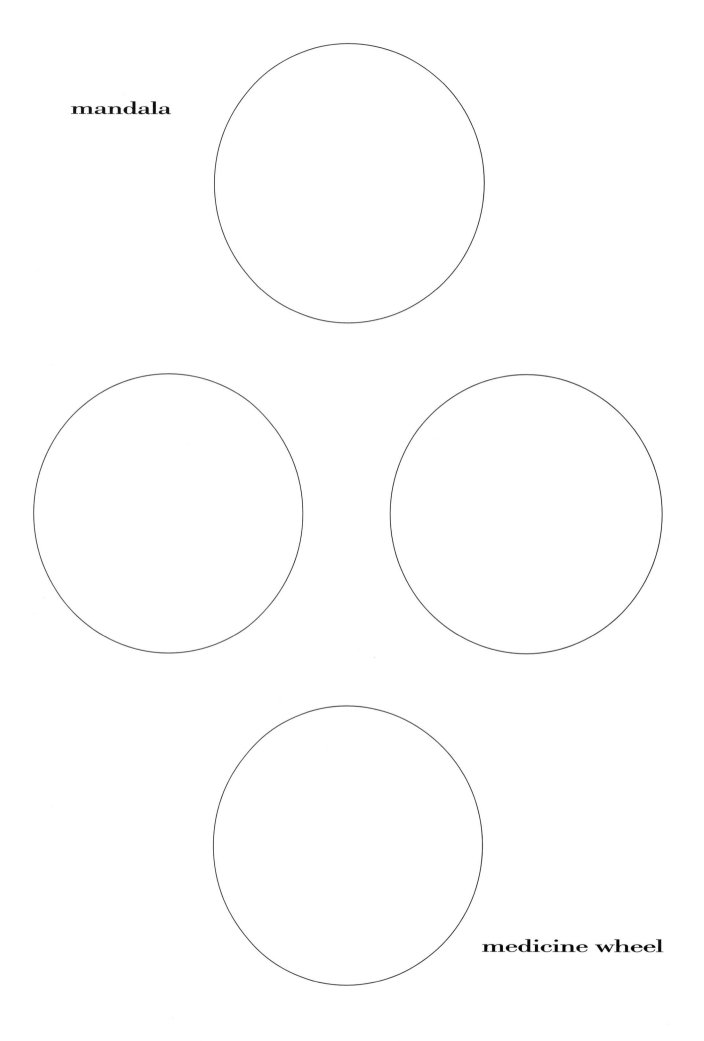

mandala

medicine wheel

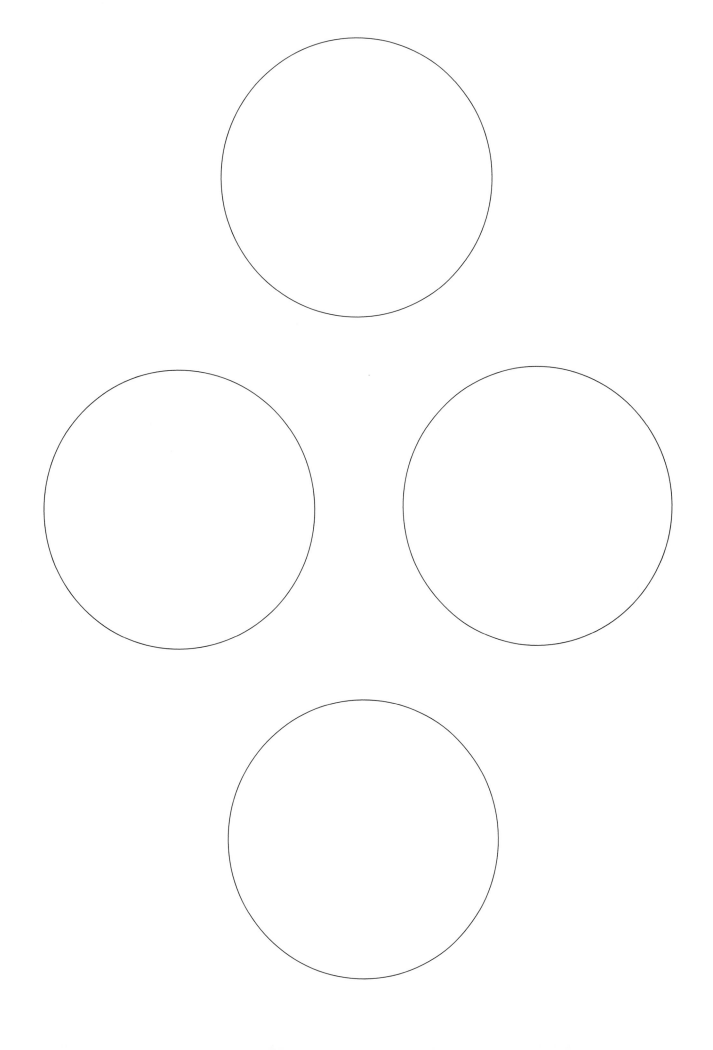

Journaling and Dream Work

Another useful technique is to begin a journal. It might be a dream journal in which you faithfully record the deep longing and messages of other dimensions and levels of SELF. Perhaps it is a journal of your feelings and thoughts as you move through your days. Inform family and friends that they may not enter this private domain without your permission. Your journal is a sacred space in which you can openly and honestly express your Self and uncover "who" you are.

I personally find journal writing to be an effective tool. It continually provides a place of safety and a space for honesty. I'd like to share a passage I wrote when my last two children went off to college. In the passage below, I had boldly embraced the positive, while trying to deny the shadow side of that moment. It symbolized a closing of a special stage of my life, and I was having difficulty acknowledging its loss and impact.

> August 4th: "I am looking forward to more freedom as my children move into the world. I don't intend to stop mothering - just need to let go and not be available 24 hrs/day. My children seem equally ready, as they begin school in different cities. I had really expected to be depressed or anxious - or to hang on, but I'm not feeling any pain - only joy. I've yearned to do my own growing and venturing into new experiences. I'm even feeling that it is O.K. to feel this joy and relief. Whoops - just a momentary sense of anxiety at all the time and freedom that's mine. I'm suddenly feeling a bit lonely and empty. Swallow hard, breathe... O.K., so it will take awhile to enjoy my joy. I guess I'm feeling some loss. You can't be a mother for 26 years and not feel something. It's a big change. I need some time to embrace it. I don't have to do it all at once. Whew!"

Journal writing is often a first step toward acceptance and self-realization. It is here that we begin to encounter both our shadow and our wisdom. Over time, we perceive the recurring themes, patterns, and ideas that shape our lives, as well as the ways in which we have grown. For more ambitious individuals, writing your personal story or mythology can help place the events and experiences of your life into a more expanded context, allowing them to address the larger themes, archetypes, and myths that speak through you.

Dream Work

The world of dreams is as real to the dreamer as our everyday world of space-time and matter. Past, present, and future blend effortlessly into one another in this ethereal realm. Important scientific discoveries as well as novels have been born here. In 1865, German Chemist August Kekulé puzzled over the chemical structure of benzene. Then one night, he had a strange dream. He saw a circle created by a snake biting its own tail. Upon awakening, Kekulé realized that the snake was symbolically showing him that the structure of benzene was cyclic in nature.[12] Author Richard Bach received the idea for his book *Jonathan Livingston Seagull* in a dream. Amazingly, the world of dreams offers information, knowledge, and wisdom not yet known or consciously recognized in our world of physicality. Information and endless possibilities are always available; all we have to do is ask. Dreams often tell us about our health, our families, and coming events; we need to pay attention.

I encourage you to keep a dream journal next to your bed. It will reveal recurrent themes and patterns, and may even help you stay healthy or find a new job. Try it for several weeks; discover the treasures hidden in your own dreams.

MEDITATION AND SPIRITUAL PRACTICE

It is healing to go on retreat. Quiet places and moments help us re-examine our lives, our values, and our priorities. In silence, we are able to hear our Selves, and we become aware of what wants to grow and change in our lives. All we need do is listen.

Some people experience their purpose by joining a community of service. Whether it is an ashram, the peace corps, or assisting in schools or hospitals, many feel a spiritual joy and realize fulfillment through the gift of giving. Through helping others, they help themselves. They find a healthy context and perspective in which to experience their lives.

Those who feel a deep dedication and commitment to a spiritual pathway or tradition might embrace a spiritual practice. Such pathways assist with the deep work of Spirit and guide individuals in the exploration of non-physical realms and domains. One need not be a monk or a nun to participate in a spiritual practice. A practice can begin with meditation and dialogue with a guru or guide.

Spiral-Meditation of St. Ignatius of Loyola

St. Ignatius of Loyola often used this spiritual exercise to intensify and enrich his meditative practice:

"I will remain quietly meditating upon the point in which I have found what I desire without any eagerness to go on till I have been satisfied."[13]

St. Ignatius emphasized the importance of returning to specific parts of prayer and meditation for the purpose of deepening and enriching the experience. In some instances, an individual repeats a meditation or prayer that has given rise to painful reflections and feelings. On other occasions, the prayer of repetition may return one to a moment of ecstatic vision or happiness. Whatever the emotion or the experience, St. Ignatius encourages us to return to the particular words, feelings, and ideas that convey intense or significant meaning in order to fully embrace its message. He tells us that through repetition, we attain new levels of acceptance and growth. Each insight deepens our understanding and our relationship with the Divine. Every time we hear anew a prayer, a symphony, a poem, or see the same movie, we become aware of different layers and nuances of meaning not previously recognized. Each repetition offers us a new treasure.

"Method

+ Recall the feelings of the first period of prayer.
+ Use, as a point of entry, the scene, word, or feeling that was previously most significant.
+ Allow the Spirit to direct the inner movements of your heart during this time of prayer."[14]

St. Ignatius urges us to work through such moments, rather than to avoid places of stuckness and pain. Each repetition carries the petititoner and/or meditator to a different level of understanding and awareness. By spiraling around, on ever higher planes of consciousness, we deepen and transform our pain, joy, emptiness, and gnosis. I encourage you to try this with your favorite prayer or meditation.

Spiritual Rituals of Native Americans

Variations of these techniques are found throughout the world among earth's indigenous peoples. All help individuals attain an altered state of consciousness, purify their consciousness, and embrace ASOUL.

Smudging

Before a person can be healed or heal another, they need to physically and spiritually purify themselves of negative energy or bad spirits. Indigenous peoples burn herbs and grasses in a ritual of purification called smudging.

To do a smudging ceremony, burn dried sage in a stone or clay bowl. Begin with a prayer to the Creator and ask the spirits for help. Next, rub your hands in the smoke and direct the smoke to any area of your body in need of spiritual healing. Gather the smoke into your body several times, praying all the while for healing and purification. One person may smudge a group of people, using hands or a feather to disperse the smoke. Oftentimes, sage is used first, followed by cedar. Sweetgrass, at the close of this ceremony, will call forth good influences and spirits. Smudging invites plant power into our lives; it is essential to give respect and honor to these spirits. We must treat them well.[15,16]

Sweatlodge

The sweatlodge (inipi) is used for purification, prayer, and spiritual awakening. The entrance to the sweatlodge traditionally faces west toward the setting sun, a symbol of renewal and rebirth. Symbolically, each person enters into the womb of the Great Mother and sits upon a bed of sage. Twelve rocks are heated to extremely high temperatures and placed in a firepit. Before pouring water over the hot stones, a medicine person sings traditional chants and prayers. Steam fills the lodge and heat reaches extremely high levels. In order to withstand this intense heat, it is often necessary to alter one's state of consciousness. Strange events have been reported to occur during medicine ceremonies in sweatlodges, attesting to the presence of powerful spirit beings.[15,16]

Vision Quests

Visions quests (hanblecheyapi) are experiences of intense self-reflection, an inward journey which brings an individual into direct confrontation with nature and Self. The individual is challenged to spiritually awaken from darkness in order to live in the light. Revelation is vision quest's special gift, signifying self-actualization and rebirth into an expanded state of consciousness.

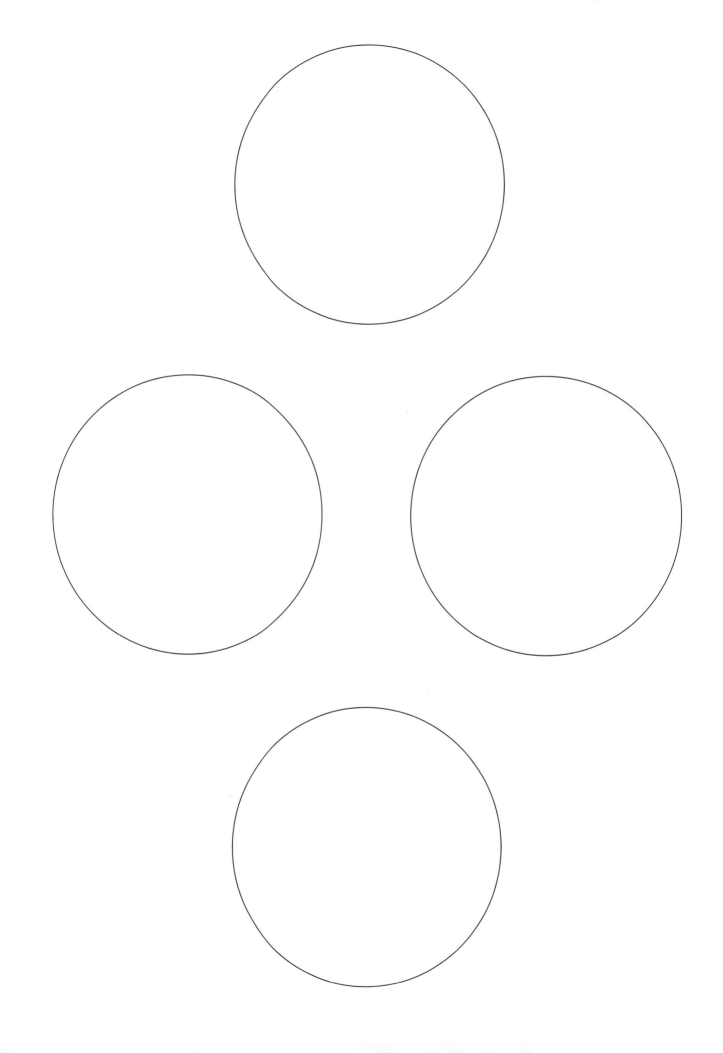

Visions quests are still performed today. It is customary to offer tobacco and other gifts to various spirits and guides, to construct your own questing place, to undergo a sweatlodge purification, as well as to fast and to pray for several days and nights. Inviting a Medicine person to guide your journey is wise. He/She can help you discern the full meaning and purpose of your vision quest.[15,16]

Medicine Wheel

Mandalas of India and Tibet, stone circles of Europe, and medicine wheels of Native Americans are hoops of great power and transformation. Mandalas represent the Sacred Circle and the Hoop of Many Nations to which humankind must ultimately return.[15,16] Wheels teach us how to live in balance and harmony with Mother Earth and Father Sky.

This sentiment is reflected in the following Ojibuay prayer.

"Grandfather, look at our brokenness. We know that in all creation only the human family has strayed from the Sacred Way. We know that we are the ones who are divided and we are the ones who must come back together to walk in the Sacred Way. Grandfather, Sacred One, teach us love, compassion and honor that we may heal the earth and heal each other."[17]

Medicine wheels enfold ancient traditions of education, culture, healing, purification, and spiritual awakening. We enter the medicine wheel from the South and slowly walk clockwise around the sacred circle. We address the Four Directions (north, east, south, and west), the Four Nations (white, red, yellow, and black), the Four Seasons (winter, spring, summer, and fall) as well as the Four Stages of Life (birth, youth, adult, and elder). Rituals, ceremonies, and symbols of the Medicine Wheel convey wisdom, transmute understanding, and transform all who follow its teachings.

The Sacred Pipe

During my visit to the Lakota Nation, on Turtle Island, my husband and I were invited to join the Sacred Hoop of Many Nations. All present formed a large circle; we smudged and cleansed ourselves with the smoke of a cedar branch. As we stood, we silently spoke our prayers. We quietly watched as the spiritual leader of the Lakota peoples lit the sacred pipe. We realized that this was an important moment in humankind's history. It represented the mending of our planet and the joining of all nations.

I watched the smoke rise in the bowl of the pipe and heard the ancient prayers of many nations fill our circle. We all yearned for peace, harmony, and the restoration of our planet. We were filled with longing as well as despair. Was there enough time to heal our beautiful planet? Would humanity draw together and recognize that we are one people enjoined in the seamless fabric of life? Could we mend our ways of war and violence and learn, instead, to live in peace with all nations?

Once upon a time, humankind traveled outwardly to all corners of our planet. Now, however, all nations must return to the sacred circle in peace. Would... Could humankind make this evolutionary transition and embrace a peace-loving, sustainable way of life with Mother Earth, Father Sky, and all species who dwell upon our planet? Will we grow to understand that we are one species which comes in many colors, cultures, religions, and perspectives? These were the poignant questions that each of us was asking as we awaited our turn to smoke the sacred pipe. Once upon a time, we had exhaled the Breath of the Invisible. Once upon a second time, we, again, must inhale this sacred energy if we wish to survive.

After the elders in the center of the circle prayed and smoked the pipe, they began to pass it around the circle. The first to smoke it was a woman. I watched and observed how the others before me were smoking the pipe. I wanted to do it correctly, so that I would not offend my hosts. I wanted to add my energy and prayers to those of my brothers and sisters in this special circle. Finally, it was my turn. I proudly turned to accept the sacred pipe from an elder. I closed my eyes and took three gentle puffs of smoke from the pipe and let it pour out through my nostrils and throat. Soothing and comforting smoke filled my being. Satisfied, I turned and handed the pipe to my husband. I watched as he too drew the Breath of the Invisible into his heart and Soul.

We watched as the sacred pipe made its way, one by one, around the circle. We were One with the Invisible and we were deeply moved by this ancient ceremony. Slowly, we left the circle and began to dance. The beat of the drums and the ancient words echoed through my heart. I felt that I had, once again, returned home.

THE ART OF LAUGHING AND CRYING (PSYCHONEUROIMMUNOLOGY)

"To everything there is a season... a time to laugh and a time to weep."[18] Tears are nature's medicine. Our tears express feelings of relief, fear, pain, joy, and sadness. People who are unable to express their pain or sorrow keep their emotions locked inside; often they become depressed. We cannot withhold anger and sadness without restraining joy and happiness. They are linked together, as two sides of a coin. In order to become whole, we must share our pain as well as our joy. We must learn to cry, to laugh, to accept and, ultimately, to let go. Only then are we free to move on with our lives. Norman Cousins knew the healing value of laughter and joy, and personally healed himself, against all odds, with mirth and merriness.[19]

Tears of sadness chemically differ from tears of joy. Astonishingly, all our emotions and thoughts seem to have distinct biochemical signatures. An emerging new field known as psychoneuroimmunology indicates that mental depression can also depress one's immune system. Depression is an important factor in the onset and course of illness. Sustained arousal fosters cardiovascular disease, impairs DNA repair, and slows production of various immune system components. Not surprisingly, the biochemical effects of our positive attitudes, beliefs, emotions, and life-serving strategies increase the healing of wounds, tissue repair, and the likelihood that one gets well and stays well. Many neuropeptides also serve as biological mediators of emotion. And in ways not fully understood, ceremonies, rituals, prayer, meditation, transcendental and spiritual experience enhance and potentiate the healing process. Through the practice of psychoneuroimmunology, we learn the importance of both laughing and crying. We attain wholeness whenever the healing powers of mind, body, and spirit blend together. A new era of healing and medicine has begun.

The next three vignettes illustrate how our attitudes and beliefs shape our responses to various situations and challenges.

Life is a Traffic Jam

Every one of us has been caught in a traffic jam at one time or another. What would you do? How do you think you would react if you learned that you would be delayed for at least one-half hour? Let us look at the way two different drivers chose to handle this unexpected situation.

Driver 1 instantly begins to cuss and fuss. He "berates himself" with a flurry of demeaning statements: "I'm really stupid. I should have left earlier. I could have taken another route." He has a whole litany of "shoulds, coulds, don'ts and musts." None of this is of any help. Rather, it's a perfect way to elevate blood pressure, exacerbate an ulcer, and lower self-esteem. Driver 1, having determined the realities of his situation, is now fully convinced that he will be fired from his job, fail to pay his mortgage, his children won't go to college... and eventually, his wife will leave him. Exasperated and exhausted, Driver 1 doesn't realize that traffic is moving again, until the honking of car horns jars him back to his senses. He arrives at his office haggard and frazzled, and still deeply involved in his own internal processes and thoughts. He pays little attention to his client or boss. You guessed it. The meeting fulfills his worst fears and ends unsuccessfully. (The movie "Falling Down" with Michael Douglas is an extreme case in point.)

Now let us consider Driver 2's response to the same traffic jam. He knows he will be late to an important meeting. However, Driver 2 avoids the negative commentary of Driver 1. Instead, Driver 2 makes use of this time to meditate, to listen to music, or to consider his strategies when he arrives at his meeting. He might also find the insanity of the other drivers around him amusing as well as sad. Rather than "break down," Driver 2 chooses to relax and enjoy the "break" the traffic jam has presented to him. When traffic resumes, Driver 2 is calm, refreshed, and ready to go. Yes, Driver 2's meeting is a success. So is his response to the traffic jam.

Drivers 1 and 2 are really you and me. All of us experience many unpleasant situations in our daily lives. The way we handle these events often determines the quality, even the length of our lives. What will you do the next time you're in a traffic jam?

Empathy

Most of us have never considered what it is like to live in a wheelchair or sustain a lifelong disability. The following experience taught me to appreciate my body and all that it allows me to do.

On New Year's Day, I was admitted to St. John's Hospital. My left foot was swollen and throbbing with pain. I had no idea what was causing my distress. All too rapidly, I found myself in the O.R., surrounded by a hastily summoned surgical team. No one was quite sure what to expect. Hours later, when I awakened, my left leg was wrapped in a knee-high cast. Several bones had been shattered, necessitating a bone graft from heel to sole. It would be at least three months until I would be able to again walk on my foot.

As the day drew to a close, I was wheeled to my car. Once home, the reality of coping with this unforeseen event began to sink in. Suddenly, the downstairs den became my entire world. Exhausted, I slowly drifted to sleep, wrapped in pain and disbelief.

Gradually, the pain diminished and I learned how to deal with my injury, my limitations, and life in a wheelchair. A physical therapist taught me to climb a few steps and how to use a walker. Suddenly, my world grew larger. Soon, I was courageous enough to venture out into the larger world. I was ecstatic.

Suddenly, I became a "we." In order to go anywhere, I needed an assistant. Independence was but a dim memory. I had to learn patience, to ask for everything I needed or wanted, and to plan every move hours before leaving home. It would not be easy to return home, even for essentials. In retrospect, I realized the incredible freedom that two healthy legs had always provided me. Yet, never before had I stopped to thank them for effortlessly transporting me from place to place.

Have you ever been confined to a wheelchair? Maybe you, too, could not accomplish even the simplest chore without assistance. Perhaps you still depend on others to make your way in the world. Having walked in your shoes, I better understand your world and empathize with your dilemmas and your courage; these have also become my challenges and my world. For a period of time, I joined your noble ranks. You are my heros and heroines.

It might be helpful to your own process to assist someone who is disabled, handicapped, elderly, or infirmed. Perhaps you can brighten their lives by bringing them a plant, providing lunch, or just sitting quietly alongside your new friend.

Caretakers

Many of us have discovered that we are members of the "sandwich generation," responsible for the care of our aging parents as well as our growing children. Constantly involved with the care and feeding of others, we have little time or energy left to meet our personal needs.

Attending a support group for the frequently overwhelmed caretaker is a good place to start your own healing process. Recognizing that you are not the only one in this position enables you to feel less victimized. Less resentment helps you mobilize your efforts more effectively. Group participation prevents your further isolation from family, friends, and the rest of your community. Other members of your group will tell you about available resources and where to get needed help. There is no need to do everything alone. By prioritizing your efforts and goals, you can meet some of your own needs. By replenishing and caring for yourself, you actually become a better caretaker to others.

Gradually acknowledge your own limitations. Begin to delegate a few responsibilities to others by learning to gracefully say "no." Admit that you cannot be everything to everyone. Try to evaluate your motivations for helping and begin to recognize the ways you allow yourself to become overly involved. Identify your guilts, your fears, and your areas of vulnerability. Why do you have such trouble setting limits? Who is really taking care of whom?

Let those in your care do as much as they can for their own well-being. A good caretaker encourages autonomy, choice, and independence. Choice is truly magical for it always empowers.

A wise caretaker remembers to empower him or herself. Take some time for your own healing and rejuvenation. Remember that you are a person first and a caretaker second. If you take care of yourself, as well as those dependent upon you, you will be less overwhelmed and less resentful. For some, a quiet leisurely bath is restorative. Others might prefer an evening out with friends, a drive in the country, or a walk on the beach. When we learn to take care of ourselves as well as others, caretaking becomes a spiritual service, a chance to grow, and a true expression of love.

A MIRACLE

People from all walks of life, all ages, and all ethnic backgrounds often surprise their doctors, families, and even themselves... by getting well, against all odds. I'd like to share this special story of courage and blessing. Dreams do come true and miracles do happen.

Alice's Story

Alice is a special lady whose wisdom lies on the other side of words. Alice is 57 years old and lives in California. She is my identical twin.

Nearly twenty years ago, Alice sustained a serious head injury while teaching a physical education class to high school students. Following this accident, her life was never the same. She tried many times to return to teaching, but found that she could not. Her doctors were unable to effect a cure and so, Alice sadly took a disability retirement, divorced her husband, and remained at home.

Five years ago, as I prepared for a holiday get-together in my home, Alice arrived at the door with lip dangling and leg dragging. I stared at her in horror. I immediately called her doctor and arranged to bring Alice to the hospital the next morning. The next day, after extensive testing, doctors determined that Alice had a brain tumor in the left frontal lobe. They scanned her all over, and fortunately no other cancer was discovered. A biopsy revealed the nature of the cancer and radiation therapy was the treatment of choice. Alice was given a prognosis of one week to three months; she returned home to die. The radiation effected a cure that was to last four and one-half years. Alice smiled. She always knew she would live.

Then last November, Alice informed me she was almost "cured" since four and one-half years had already passed since the tumor was first discovered. She was on the home stretch and close to the five year mark. Our family began to breathe a bit easier.

A week later, on Thanksgiving Day, Alice arrived at my home. I was surprised to see her in a wheelchair, but I was aware she had experienced some recent difficulty in walking. She also seemed quite lethargic, but the busyness of the holiday and the arrival of my other guests kept me from concern. Following dinner, one of my sons and my friend, Father Peter, offered to help me take Alice home. We managed to get her into my small, compact car, but encountered enormous difficulty in taking her out of it. Suddenly, all three of us realized that Alice was frightened and near panic. We all began to suspect Alice was paralyzed from the waist-down. It took five of us to finally transfer Alice from my car into her home. After the inital shock, I contacted her neurologist and arranged to transfer her to a hospital the next morning.

The next day, we learned Alice had a second tumor, this time on the right side of the brain. A biopsy revealed that it was the same type of tumor that she had had previously, and that very little in the way of treatment was available. She could not have any more radiation, and we learned that chemotherapy was not likely to be successful for her type of cancer. Together, Alice and our family determined there was nothing else, medically, to do for her. Again, Alice was sent home to die.

Alice was very depressed. Depression also echoed and reverberated through our entire family. Alice was reluctantly transferred to a skilled nursing facility when her condition deteriorated, and she became more depressed. Several months passed and her prognosis indicated 3-6 months of life; no more. Alice did not want to die. I suggested that she visualize a pink "pac-man" devouring the cancer cells and cleaning up the debris. "Couldn't hurt, and there are absolutely no bad side effects," I offered. This seemed to be the only type of treatment available. It made all of us feel there was still room for hope. With great sadness, I contacted Hospice and arranged for their assistance.

As soon as Hospice came on the scene, Alice's demeanor changed. No longer depressed nor lethargic, she suddenly began to fight back. She was determined to live and to return home. She wouldn't hear of any other idea and steadfastly and resolutely held to her goals. Everyone noticed an immediate change in behavior. A few months passed, and Alice seemed not only emotionally better, but also physically better. She was more interactive and alert, and her cognitive processes were returning, intact. Everyone sensed something was happening. We contacted her doctors and arranged for another MRI to ascertain her status.

Following the MRI, I was informed that this second tumor had disappeared. I couldn't believe it and was afraid to share the news with Alice, fearful that it was somehow a mistake. To quell my fears, the doctors agreed to do a second MRI a few weeks later. And, once again, there was no evidence of any brain tumor on the MRI. Alice had an "SRC" (spontaneous remitted cancer). A miracle had truly transpired.

I was delighted to share the news with my twin. She didn't seem too surprised. She had suspected that she was healing. Still, she shyly shared that she did not know how she got well. I suggested that an unconscious part of personhood knows how to heal and cure us, while the conscious Self does not. Alice was incredibly positive and determined to be healed, although she did not know if it was possible. We decided to thank the part of her that had allowed her to heal. She had received a blessing.

Alice is continuing to surprise everyone. Paralyzed from the waist-down since Thanksgiving, it seemed most unlikely that she would ever walk again. But Alice is determined to see what is possible. With the help of the nursing staff and her physical therapist, Alice can now move her legs. She is not quite able to walk alone, but she can transfer herself from bed to wheelchair and back. It is enough to allow her to return home. Alice smiles. She knew she would not die and that she would, one day, return home. She just knew.

Importantly, there is thorough and ample documentation of Alice's second tumor and follow-up MRIs that trace its progress and final disappearance. Doctors are totally amazed and unable to say what enabled a miracle to occur. When you see Alice, though, she shyly smiles. She is going home!

GRIEF WORK

Death as Process

So much of our lives revolves around the mystery, apprehension, and fear of death. We go to great lengths to prolong life. We do everything to retard the aging process and to stave off death. Yet each of us will experience personal loss during our lifetime, and each of us will ultimately experience our own death. Still, most of us are ill prepared to deal with the death of our loved ones, and even less prepared to confront our own mortality. And yet, illness, diversity, and grief are often harbingers of personal change and growth. Why seek only to ease our pain and to numb our grief? Growth and transformation come when we open ourselves to the positive, healing potential of illness and loss. Rather, death, as the culmination of life, brings closure to worldly challenges, a search for new understanding, and the promise of resurrection.

But it is not only the ill and elderly who are dying. Africa is losing its young to famine and starvation. Millions, worldwide, are dying from HIV+ disease, and our planetary population is graying in such great numbers that it is straining our welfare and medical systems. Hence, all nations and most families will face the necessity of coming to terms with death, whether they wish to or not. Death intensifies and deepens our relationships and potentiates the value of all life. One can choose to collapse into despair and hopelessness, or one can choose to deal with their disease and to learn to live more fully.

A Grief Story

Grief and death are normal processes. They are part of the cycle of life. We journey from Self to SELF, from love to Love, and life to Life. Below is a 49-year-old woman's grief story.[20]

"My father died of a heart attack and my mother died of cancer. My father's death was a surprise and a shock, and my mother's death was a long ordeal. I know that people sometimes think that a sudden and quick death is easier, but for me it was important to talk with my mother and even just to sit and hold her hand, and though those last weeks and months were hard, I'm grateful we had them. With my father there was no time to say good-bye. I wish there had been."

Perhaps none of us can be fully ready for the death of our loved ones. But we can strive to live each moment with integrity and as fully as possible. We can speak our truths, release our anger, and be a source of comfort and strength to those we love. We must learn to affirm life, even in our dying.

Ruach

Acceptance of death comes only after a period of mourning, which may last months or even years.

We named our all-white Russian Wolfhound, Ruach. "Ruach" is a Hebrew word; it means the breath of the invisible as well as the Spirit of the Heart. Whenever you looked into his eyes, you embraced the wisdom of eternity.

Six months ago, Ruach came to live with my family. At first he was frightened and restrained. He warmed up to us only gradually. Eventually, Ruach and our other dog, Bright Star, became lifetime friends.

A few days after his first birthday, Ruach underwent a simple surgical procedure. He was up and about in a few hours, and returned home the same day. Ruach was glad to see his playmate, and we were happy he was well. Four days later, my husband, Gilbert, was in our garden, pruning his roses. Suddenly, he heard a shrill cry of pain and turned to see what had happened. Gilbert saw Ruach lying on the ground, unconscious. Bright Star was standing beside her fallen friend; she knew something was terribly wrong. Bright Star lay down next to Ruach and began to wail and moan.

Gilbert and our son, Bruce, quickly drove Ruach to the vet. Both were in a state of disbelief and shock. Sadly, the vet told them Ruach had died. He said something about an aneurysm or a spinal embolus, or even a delayed effect of the anesthesia. Gilbert and Bruce never heard what the doctor had said. They were too filled with anguish and pain. Everything had happened so fast, and nothing was making any sense.

Thanks to the sensitivity of Gilbert and Bruce, I had a chance to say one last good-bye to Ruach. All of us cried and shook our heads in disbelief. At home, the house seemed strangely empty and quiet. Nothing seemed real.

We all moved slowly and with great effort during the next few days. We went through our hours and days as if we were robots. Some of us cried, some expressed anger, and others remained numb. And each day, at the exact moment of Ruach's untimely death, his loyal companion Bright Star would lie down upon the very spot where Ruach passed away. She, too, seeks to understand the incomprehensible.

My friend, Jane, sent me this poem after her sister's death. I found it soothing and comforting.

"To Those I Love and Those Who Love Me"

When I am gone, release me, let me go
    I have so many things to see and do
You mustn't tie yourself to me with tears...
    Be happy that we had so many years.
I gave to you my love. You can only guess
    How much you gave to me in happiness.
I thank you for the love you each have shown
    But now it is time I traveled on alone.
So grieve awhile for me if grieve you must
Then let your grief be confronted by trust.

It is only for a while that we must part
So bless the memories of the heart.
I won't be far away. For life goes on.
So if you need me, call and I will come
Though you can't see me or touch me I'll be near...
And if you listen with your heart you'll hear

All of my love around you soft and clear.
And then, when you must come this way alone
I'll greet you with a smile and
'Welcome Home.'[21]

Learning to Forgive

This is the story of Elhom. She had married at the age of 16 and moved to the Middle East with her husband. The first years of their marriage were happy ones. Their joy increased with the birth of a beautiful son. But slowly the fabric of their marriage began to unravel, and Elhom's husband of eight years divorced her. Bewildered and angry, Elhom returned to the United States.

Elhom's ex-husband refused to support Elhom and their son. Life was very hard. She worked as a manicurist to support herself and her child as best she could. Her ex-husband remarried and never again visited his first-born son. Elhom was outraged. There was little joy in her life.

Shortly after her ex-husband's new marriage, Elhom noticed a lump in her breast. A biopsy revealed cancer; surgery gave Elhom the promise of renewed life. No longer able to support or care for her son, Elhom wrote her ex-husband for child support and assistance. He again refused. He accused Elhom of faking illness in order to gain his financial help. Elhom passively gave up. Her health continued to decline.

Several months later, Elhom called me from her hospital room. She was dying and wanted to see me one last time. She expressed concern for her son and worried what would become of him after she died. I helped her arrange for his care and education. She looked more peaceful. Then Elhom told me that she had received a visit from her ex-husband. He seemed surprised, as well as shocked, to see her hooked up to so many tubes and hospital equipment. He suddenly realized that Elhom was really dying. He begged Elhom's forgiveness for the way he had treated her and their son. As he opened the door to leave, Elhom shared her thoughts with the man she still loved. She told him that she would forgive him only if she died. But if she recovered and returned home, they would have to do a considerable amount of healing before she would really be able to forgive him. And then he was gone. Still the loving, caring wife, Elhom forgave her ex-spouse. She died a few hours later.

The act of for-give-ness releases blame, pain, victimhood, past deeds, and judgment. Although one forgives, the lessons learned are remembered always. Now we continue our journeys with deeper understanding and greater empathy, and less burden. Whenever we for-give, we receive grace. "To err is human, to forgive Divine."[22]

RITUALS AND RITES OF PASSAGE

Myths are the stories, ceremonies, customs, and rituals which shape our individual and collective lives. Through myths and stories, we re-connect with the mysteries of Universe.

Myth, rituals, and rites of passage take place in sacred space and time, celebrate life's journeys and transitions, and proclaim our growth and evolution from one level to another. Myths, rituals, and ceremonies tell us Who We Are. They shape our relationships, heal our losses, express our deepest beliefs, bind peoples together, and celebrate our very existence. Indeed, sacred myths and rituals are fundamental and integral to individual, family, community, and Universe.

Creating Your Own Rituals

We take part in many rituals and ceremonies simply by being members of certain nations, cultures, and religions. Such occasions include national holidays (Martin Luther King, Jr. Day), religious holy-days (Christmas, Ramadan), as well as national remembrances (Cinco de Mayo, July 4th, Thanksgiving Day, Memorial Day). To create your own rituals, first define the particular occasion you wish to celebrate. Is it seasonal, annual, or will any time of year do? Celebrations at dusk and dawn always convey a sense of mystery; it is here that day and night meet. Is your occasion public (graduation, grand opening of a store) or private (wedding, divorce, anniversary)? Determine if location and hour are important. Are special clothes a part of this ceremony (wedding dress, graduation gown)?

Next, decide what you want to say and would like to do at your ceremony. Simple, heart-felt sharing is all you really need to personalize any occasion. And remember, rituals can also occur spontaneously. They arise from the very depths of your being.

A Piece of Apple Pie—Allen

One of my clients, Allen, recalls a family ritual that occurred whenever an event of great importance would take place. His immigrant parents were poor, and seldom had the money to spend on extras. But at special times of celebration, they would note the occasion by sharing a slice of apple pie. This ritual sharing became the symbol of good fortune, achievement, success, and anything out of the ordinary that happened in the family. A slice of apple pie assumed an importance of its own.

When Allen was graduated from sixth grade, nearly 40 years ago, he was overjoyed. It was a wondrous moment for him and his family. Still, Allen didn't quite realize its full significance until his parents invited him to share a slice of apple pie with them, and revealed that neither of them had ever gone beyond fourth grade in school. He had accomplished what they never did, and in so doing, his parents felt a personal sense of achievement and great pride. A slice of apple pie deeply enriched the entire family's joy and understanding of this special moment. After all these years, the ritual and symbol live on for Allen; its importance and emotional meaning shine through his tear-filled eyes and are reflected in his smile, as he recounts his first recognition of the power of myth. Rituals and rites enable us to experience completeness and closure, to let go, and to move on.

Age Obsession

As I approached my fiftieth birthday, I became obsessed with the issue of age and aging. At 40, society had already determined that I was "over the hill." Naturally, I worried about the significance of reaching 50. Was I old and soon to be discarded, forgotten, or...?

I explored the meaning of "age" in every possible context. Geologically, our planet experienced the Mezoic and Cenosoic Eras long before humankind walked upon the earth. In fact, earth has passed through ice ages, dark ages, golden ages, the bronze age, the iron age, the age of enlightenment, and the age of reason. Presently, humanity looks with hope to a New Age and a New Millennium.

Many people collect ancient artifacts with great enthusiasm. They speak glowingly and reverently of ancient cultures. Even old furniture and antiques are regarded with great respect and sold for high prices, simply because they are old.

Culturally, we speak of young age, teen-age, middle age, old age, and "coming of age." And we only become Sage and Crone upon reaching age 56. So why does our society consider a woman over 40 and a man over 50 "over the hill"? Why do we ignore and abandon people at the very summit of their lives? Why not value our elders as much as we do old furniture and relics? And why not encourage our elders to share their knowledge and experience with the rest of us? Humankind would be greatly enriched if we did. And why wait until middle age to realize the sacred in all things?

Let us seize this moment and proclaim the wisdom of Crone and Sage that dwells within each of us.

Celebrating the Wise Woman (Crone) and Sage

I have adapted this rite of passage from "The Grandmother of Time."[23] Feel free to change and modify my ideas to suit your personal tastes and needs.

When you are 56 or more years old, you are ready to enter the age of wisdom. Modern society devalues the aging process, while emphasizing the joys and carefreeness of youth; little wonder so many men and women fail to honor and celebrate this momentous occasion.

Invite loving friends to join your celebration. Ask a friend to bring a purple jewel that will be presented to you as part of this ancient ritual. Ask another friend to bring some candles and a third to bring a bell. Invite everyone to join hands and to form a circle around the Wise Women; she is our honored guest. Light the candles one at a time, and watch them impart a soft glow to this sacred space. Ask one of your guests to welcome everyone.

> "Welcome one and all. We are here to honor {name}, who has become a Wise Woman. At 56 years of age, she has entered into a privileged state of wisdom and maturity. In ancient times, as in more modern times, a Crone is the wise woman who heals, counsels, and restores harmony and peace to all who around her."

> The Wise Woman replies: "I have traveled the long road from birth to wisdom. I thank the Goddess for the seasons that have passed and I look forward to the seasons yet to come."

A friend rings the bell 56 times or more, to honor the continuity of life. Do not hurry this part of the ceremony. As you allow the bell to chime, the importance of a life well-lived and the wisdom gained is acknowledged. This is a noble moment. As the bell rings out the 56th year, all applaud the Wise Woman who has attained maturity and wisdom.

Everyone joins in chorus to bless the new Crone { name} with wishes for health, happiness, and long life.

This ritual also can be used for men once they reach their 56th birthday (or more). They are honored as sages and given the gift of a wand in celebration of this special occasion. The following words set the tone of this ceremony:

"I would like to speak of the great medicine men and shamans who served us in ancient times. They were our sages who taught us courage, compassion, and ways of peace. They are our fathers and grandfathers. Today we honor { name} as he enters the wisdom age. This magic wand will remind you of your spiritual heritage. Now you are a Sage."

The Sage replies: "I have traveled the long road from birth to Sage. I toast the good seasons passed, and greet the good seasons yet to come."

All hold hands and remain silent as the bell chimes 56 times in honor of the Sage's life. A great ovation greets the sage and the festivities begin.

The rites of the Wise Woman and the Sage restore meaning and value to our passing years. They enrich our world and honor our memories and loved ones. Through such rituals, we join our ancestors and those yet to share humankind's sojourn upon earth. And so it is... Amen.

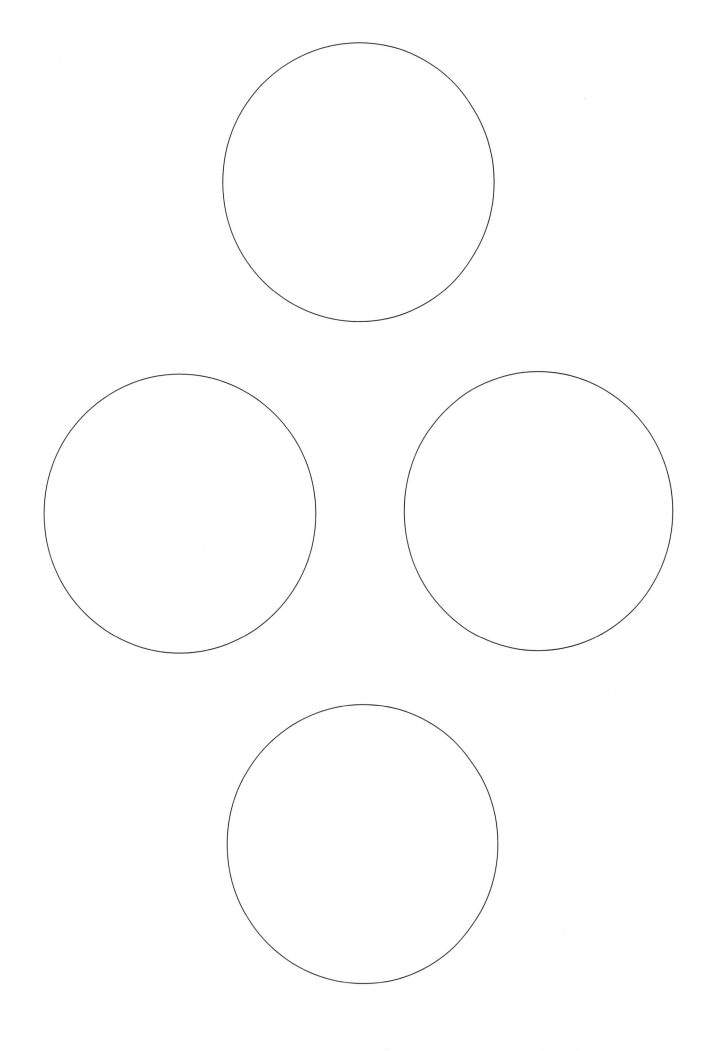

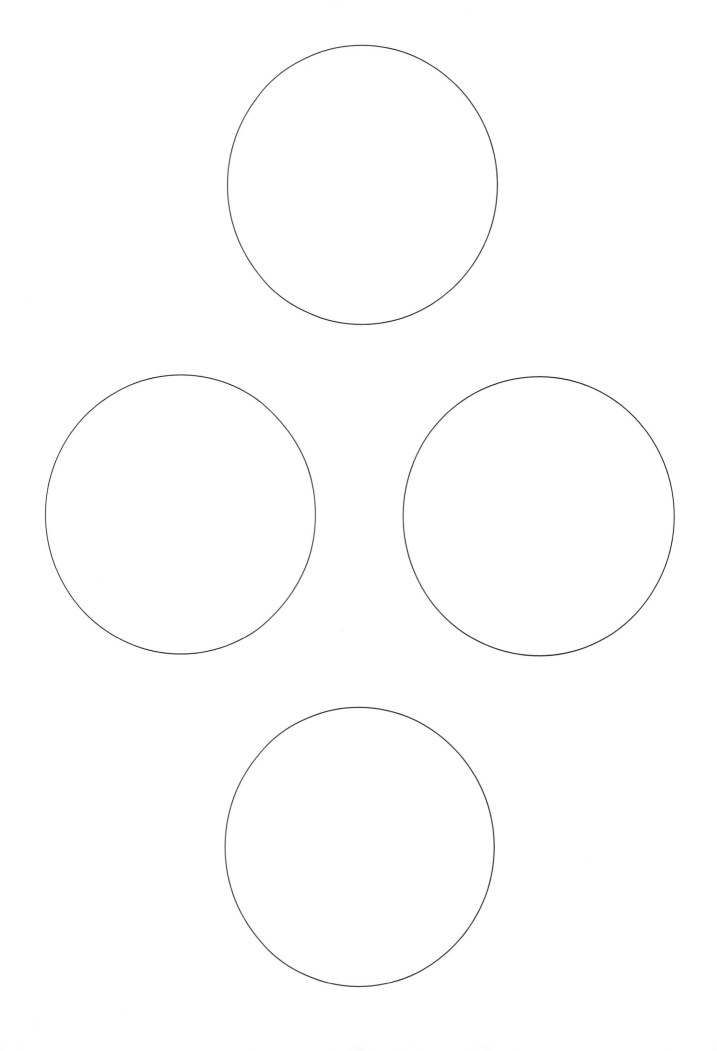

CREATING A NEW PATH

"When we go down into the well of self deeply enough we come upon the underground stream that unites all selves."[24]

Namasté emphasizes the interconnection and interrelatedness of all levels and dimensions of reality, reminding us that all creation flows from the inside-out. Blueprints and archetypal events, experiences and situations of daily life are formed in inner dimensions of Selfhood, patiently awaiting humanity's invitation into physicality. The seeds of peace dwell in our Psyches and Souls. The Path of the Heart and the paths of peace are one.

THE GENTLE WAY

I invite each of you to explore the Feminine archetypal principle which dwells within your psyche. Feminine is harbinger of inner knowing, intuition, wisdom, and working with higher purpose. She is healer, redeemer, and resurrector.

The Gentle Way recognizes the relatedness and mutual indwelling and enfolding of all levels and dimensions of existence. The Gentle Way also encourages cooperation and harmony rather than competition and exploitation; you can never gain at another's expense. The Feminine encourages you to recognize and reclaim the projections you have unconsciously placed upon others. Take responsibility for your feelings, ideas, and choices. Union of masculine and feminine psychic elements always bestows healing and wholeness. Your attainment of inner and outer peace blesses Universe with joy and harmony.

Job Description

Would you apply for this job?

Must be willing to work 70-80 hour work week, drive during rush-hour traffic, and do the work of 1.5 people. Expect to be treated as a machine rather than as a human being. Business must always take priority over family needs. Heavily stressed environment. Prepare for burn-out and stress-related disorders. Minimum benefits and holidays. No complaints, no excuses, no guarantees, no dignity. Don't call us, we'll call you... maybe.

Far too many people are working at jobs similar to the one above. Frequently, the preferred lifestyle throughout the industrialized world can only be maintained if both partners work. Yet each of us arrives home tired and exhausted at the end of the day. Dinner must be made, dishes dried, children fed and bathed, and bills paid. Many individuals also attend school in order to improve their market value. There really isn't much time or energy left over for romance, relaxation, family, or exercise. How can two exhausted partners succeed at relationship, business, or any other pursuit? The American way of business seems to oppose a "forever relationship."

We long for more time to devote to our relationships and families. Yet, the frenetic pace of our present lives leaves little time and energy to work on our important commitments to ourselves and to others. We are gradually becoming aware of the dark side of the American dream.

Edward Discovers the Gentle Way

40-year-old Edward worked for a large electronics company. His job was remarkably similar to the one described above. Fearful of losing his job due to a recessed economy, Edward began to increasingly rely upon alcohol and drugs to quell his anxiety and anger. Drugs rapidly become an addiction, threatening to destroy Edward and his family. Lucy, Edward's wife, noticed her husband's emotional withdrawal from her and their children. At first Lucy didn't realize how depressed Edward was. She was too exhausted and depressed to notice. Lucy worked 50 hours a week and carried the full responsibility for her children and household. Both Lucy and Edward were in desperate need of some relief. As Edward sank deeper into depression as well as serious drug abuse, Lucy realized she was unable to help him. As resentment between them grew, Edward found himself less willing to return home at day's end.

Edward's employer was also alarmed when a mandated test revealed that Edward was taking drugs. His company placed him in an expensive drug rehabilitation program, hoping it would effect a cure. Lucy and the children remained distant and angry; they refused to come and visit. Edward was sad, confused, and frightened. He only wished to provide for his family; he loved them.

As Edward recounted his problems to a drug counselor and talked about how tired he was, he began to cry. He realized that the very act of trying to care for his family was driving them apart. He had thought that drugs would help him endure the emotional pain of being undervalued, underpaid, and over-worked. He had needed something to help him stay awake on the job. Edward was confused and distraught. He believed that he had failed everybody: his wife, his children, his boss, even himself.

To be continued by You

I'm inviting you to decide if Edward and Lucy will learn to deal with "their" problem of substance abuse. Will Edward and Lucy learn to communicate their feelings and needs more effectively to one another? How? Should they sell their large home and move to another city where the cost of living is much lower? Is the new city safer, and can the children attend public school, rather than private school? Will reduced mortgage and household expenses allow Lucy to work part-time and have more quality time with her children? If Lucy is less haggard and tired, would she be willing to help her husband? How can Edward reduce his work load and find time to be with his family? Would Edward benefit from new job training? Is it even possible? What will happen to this family if they get a divorce?

Now that you have considered Edward and Lucy's plight, you might find it helpful to look at your own lifestyle and employment. Are you content? Do you have time to relax and to be with family and friends? Or do you arrive home nightly, so depleted and exhausted that you are unable to emotionally connect with others? What solutions will help you achieve a more harmonious, satis-fying way of life?

"In a value driven economy, the human spirit knows no limits."[25]

—Anita Roddick

RECIPE FOR A FOREVER RELATIONSHIP

Edward and Lucy learned to heal themselves and their family. Their recipe for a Forever Relationship reveals their greater understanding and awareness.

You will need equal parts of the following attributes:

Love

Commitment

Intimacy

Compassion

Acceptance

Patience

Responsibility

Forgiveness

Condiments:

1 + 1 = 3 Solutions

Willingness to Listen

Humor and Laughter

Method: Each partner freely bestows the gifts of love and a commitment to do whatever they can to help their relationship grow. Both agree that they will not give in, or give up, for they recognize that these acts are the harbingers of resentment and anger that will keep them from attaining their goal. Love and commitment form the ground of a forever relationship. From these, all else naturally flows. A gentle blending of love and commitment creates an environment of loving kindness. Trust and love always grow in a space of acceptance. Sprinkle generously with encouragement, respect, humor, and tender loving care.

Learn how to listen to your partner. Listening is love's special gift. Instead of control and manipulation, seek to resolve your differences with 1 + 1 = 3 solutions. You will always find these solutions somewhere between "my way" and "your way." Innovative solutions endow love and relationship with new insight and possibility.

Eliminate as much blame, self-righteousness, criticism, and judgment as you can. Perfection is only an illusion; do not waste time seeking perfection in yourself or others. Refrain from telling your partner how or what to be. Instead, accept your partner for who and what he or she is. Your acceptance and patience will help your partner grow. A loving heart and a forever relationship is a work-in-progress. It requires patience and a willingness to risk and share honestly and intimately with one another. Compassion and forgiveness will ease your journey and help you find your way.

Accept responsibility for your thoughts and actions. It is not fair to project them upon your lover. By reclaiming your projections, by refraining from attacking others, and by letting go of fear and inadequacy, you will move beyond ego issues and see things from a different perspective. Simply strive to be the best Self you know how to be in each moment.

Relationships reflect the highs and the lows of daily living. They tell us where we need to grow and change. Conflicts and differences are inevitable. Generously mixing an abundance of laughter and humor with sadness and pain helps maintain balance and perspective. Our emotions and problems are valuable teachers. They bestow gifts of personal transformation and spiritual awakening to those willing to share darkness and pain as well as joy and love.

Many couples are renewing their relationship with the Sacred to realize greater meaning and purpose in their lives. When couples unite with Spirit, their relationship deepens and grows; magically, new ways of love and acceptance unfold. Without relinquishing identity and Selfhood, the two of you have become as One. Lovers and Spirit blend in loving embrace; a Forever Relationship has begun.

Exercise 1

List five things that your partner does for you which make you feel loved, valued, and special.

1.

2.

3.

4.

5.

Exercise 2

List five things you do to show your partner that he/she is loved, valued, and important to you.

1.

2.

3.

4.

5.

Children need time

Children do not grow by themselves. They need love and devotion. Too many children arrive home to empty houses and exhausted parents. Children are often left to fend for themselves. We must invite our elders to serve as surrogate grandparents to our lonely children. We can also choose smaller homes, less fashionable cars, and jobs that permit at least one parent the luxury of quality time at home with their children. Consider these words by Ross Campbell, M. D.:

"Children can be conceptualized as mirrors. If love is given to them, they return it. If none is given, they have none to return. Unconditional love is reflected unconditionally, and conditional love is returned conditionally."[26]

Exercise

Determine the amount of time you spend weekly in the following activities.

Work	Sleep	Chores	Parenting	Grooming
Solitude	Recreation	Time as a Couple	School	Other

What does this exercise tell you about your own choices and priorities? Are you spending enough time with the people you love and doing the things you really enjoy?

HUMAN ECOLOGY

Although we have begun to recycle our natural resources, we have yet to develop an ecology of people. Too many people live without purpose or dignity. Disenfranchised people cry out for a rightful place in our world as well as for ways to participate in community. Recycling people affords a beneficial alternative to society's present policies of wasteful abandon of the skills, knowledge, abilities, and wisdom of earth peoples. A sacred sense of humanhood would never permit us to discard and throw away such a precious heritage.

Business Consultant Gardner expresses similar sentiments:

> "A good many of the most valuable people in any society will never burn with zeal for anything except the integrity and health and well-being of their own families—and if they achieve those goals, we need ask little more of them."[27]

Aging Into Wisdom

A friend called to invite me to the second annual Gathering of Grandmothers in Arizona. Mary Diamond told me that she had received the idea for the first and second Grandmothers' Council in a revelation. Her vision spoke about an ancient Hopi prophecy which says, *"When the Grandmothers speak, the Earth will heal."* As she described the setting and the reasons for calling the Grandmothers together, I knew that I would go.

Seventy Grandmothers, from the four corners of the world, arrived. Each shared the wisdom and knowing of her own tradition. Together, we wove a tapestry of wisdom and concern. Time is growing short and we have so much we wish to share with our younger sisters and daughters. We ask only that you open your hearts and listen to our stories.

Grandmothers reveal that old age need not be synonymous with illness, loss of vitality, loneliness, and death. Instead, Grandmothers reveal that aging is a gateway to enhanced wisdom, spiritual awakening, and personal transformation. In truth, it is a time of great generativity and creativity.

Grandmothers offer a more positive view of aging. As Grandmothers, we relinquish our earlier responsibilities of making a living and raising a family. Now, we have time for personal interests, hobbies, friends, exercise, and travel. Our wrinkles and gray hair proudly symbolize and proclaim our wisdom. We have learned that the importance and quality of life is far more important than the quantity of our days, months, and years. Realization that we do not live forever shifts our emphasis from death and aging toward embracing life more fully.

Grandmothers recognize that their lives and relationships are portions of a greater "whole"; they know that all of existence is part of Universe. Grandmothers tell us that aging is a magical and special time of life for those willing to answer Spirit's Soulful call.

The gathering also gave me cause to think about my own mother. I recalled that when I wished her "Happy Birthday," she didn't remember how old she was. I answered that she was 89 years old; Mom smiled and shyly said, "Ooh, that much." She has taught me that "old" is not a dirty word. Rather, it is the privilege of a life well lived. And I remembered another time when my friend's mother shyly told me that she was having "a bad memory day." This grandmother bravely acknowledged her limits and then continued on her way. She knows that aging bestows its own special gifts.

As the end of the gathering, we realized that dignity and purpose have returned to our Grandmothers. By fulfilling the ancient prophecy, earth has begun to heal.

We, who are presently aging into wisdom, are stretching the boundaries of mind and body. We know, from experience, how much more one enjoys life with the benefits of maturity, insight, and understanding. As guardians of our planet and of our species, Grandmothers carry the seeds and the promise of a more evolved and benevolent specieshood in humanity's future.

Humankind, individually and collectively, is maturing and age-ing. Will humanity choose to spiritually awaken? How have you lived your hours, days, weeks, and years? Are you willing to change and grow, and to embue your world with new shades, colors, and tones of elderhood?

The Dance of Shiva

Soul is timeless, ever conscious... an eternal process. Soul continually dances the endless rhythms of creation and annihilation. Humanity allows an awaiting universe to unfold. In a fundamental sense, Universe needs humankind in order to know Itself. Humanity is standing at the very edge of chaos. We must decide the future of our planet and our species. Ours is an awesome responsibility and choice.

Mystics tell us that humanity has a greater purpose and potential than presently realized. In an expanded state of awareness, there are no boundaries or separations, and one may experience communion with all forms of consciousness, animate and inanimate, manifest and unmanifest. When one views earth from vast distances of space, there are no boundaries to be seen. All existence is a seamless whole. Similarly, when one transcends into the realm of Consciousness Itself, one understands that there are "no levels, no dimensions, no higher, no lower, no sacred, and no profane... All Is One."

Old ways and paradigms are yielding to new ideas and concepts, reminding us that someday the new will also be old and require revision. Can you find the inner courage to usher in a new era? To do so means engaging the inner process of transformation, trusting that it will give birth to a brave new reality and specieshood.

"I would hate to get to the end of my life and

realize I had not lived, that I'd never dared to

take a chance to love, to explore, to realize my

best. Maybe the greatest risk in life is not to

risk. We should ask ourselves what our lives

will be like if we don't risk beginning."[28]

What risks are you willing to take? Can you realize your hopes and dreams for your future with your present way of life? Do you know where you are heading or even if you want to go there? Where would you like to be in one year, two, five?

CREATING A FUTURE SELF

This visualization takes approximately a half hour to complete. Initially, you may prefer to divide it into three parts and try one section at a time. It is helpful to tape record this visualization or ask someone to guide you through it.

Let us create a Self capable of carrying you into a future that you would like to experience. Some of you have chosen to deal with issues of relationships, intimacy, and commitment. Many are looking for new jobs and need to develop new skills along the way. A few have considered moving into a new lifestyle, or to another city. Others have decided to start a family, or perhaps, to encourage grown children to move into lives of their own. Still others want to let go of years of victimhood, in order to grow into a fuller sense of self and responsibility.

Close your eyes and find a comfortable position. Imagine yourself resting in a special or favorite place, a place where you can simply be. Know you are safe in this space! Remember, you are in control, and may end this exercise anytime you wish. Let us begin.

Take three or four deep breaths at your own pace. Feel your body and mind begin to slow down and relax. Continue to breathe slowly and rhythmically.

Feel a sense of relaxation move from your toes and heels, up your calves and into your knees. ... Let relaxation flow from your knees to your thighs, and into your pelvis, your hips and your lower back. ... Feel tension slip away from your body.

Allow this sense of relaxation and well-being to move into your chest, your upper back, and shoulders. Feel it gently slide down your arms—to your elbows, and down into your fingertips. Feel calmness spreading over your neck, your scalp, onto your face... and again over your neck and your torso. ... Allow your body to experience itself as deeply relaxed, limp and heavy.

1/2 minute of silence—experience this state of calmness.

Part A

Since the point of power resides in the present , you will invite the cooperation, wisdom, and skills of your Present Self on behalf of your Future Self. Ask your Present Self what change he/she wishes. Take some time to ascertain the area of transformation desired, and determine if you are comfortable with your choice.

1 minute silence.

If you discover that you are not ready to proceed, you might wish to explore any reticence or hesitation at this time. Honor these feelings; they are important. If you are ready to proceed, notice how it feels to approach and support your goal. Are you comfortable or apprehensive? Can you imagine yourself having achieved this goal? What would it feel like? Are you surprised, happy, elated, pleased?

1 minute silence

How would you inform someone that you have created this change in your life? Imagine yourself telling another person that you have succeeded in creating a Future Self.

1 /2 minute silence

Part B

Now that you have felt, heard, and envisioned your goal, and affirmed its success, you are ready to determine some of the steps that can actually bring you closer to your goals. Do you feel anxious or excited about initiating this change? Choose the feeling that will be most helpful in realizing your Future Self.

1 minute silence.

Notice any resistance. There is no need to resist your resistance. Simply let it be!

1/2 minute silence.

Determine your first step toward your goal. For example, if you are thinking about a new job, this step might entail writing a resume or attaining the necessary training to qualify for a different job. Take a few minutes to decide what needs to happen in order to create this Future Self.

1 1/2 minutes silence.

Now that you have an overview of what needs to happen, you can proceed to more specific tasks. Decide upon your first step. Visualize yourself taking this first step, and follow it to completion.

1 minute silence.

Pay attention to your feelings and thoughts as well as to your body. Are you comfortable or are you holding yourself back? Ascertain whether Step One is really your first task. Perhaps you have discovered that something else needs to take place before you begin. Include this new task in your plans.

1 1/2 minutes silence.

If you are satisfied with your first step, and also feel a measure of confidence that you will actually do it, you are ready to identify a second task toward your goal. Do you know what it will be? Do you need more information to determine Step Two? How do you plan to move ahead? Explore your options and choices.

1 1/2 minutes silence.

Part C

You are now ready to consider Step Three. For some of you, Step Three will not be very clear, while others will know exactly what to do next. Become aware of where you are in this process; allow it to be appropriate to the moment. Don't push too hard. Don't move faster than is comfortable for you. It is enough to simply begin and to take your Self seriously.

I minute silence.

Once again, acknowledge whatever ideas, thoughts, and feelings emerge. What are their messages? Do these ideas and feelings pull you back or do they encourage you to move toward New Selfhood? Are there feelings of apprehension and reticence, or challenge, excitement, or relief? Honor your feelings; allow them to be.

I /2 minute silence.

As you end this exercise, visualize and affirm your Future Self. See, hear, and feel what creating this goal/Future Self is like! Allow the richness and possibility of your Future Self to penetrate and flow through your entire being. How does it feel to become this Future Self?

1 minute silence.

As we prepare to close this visualization, take a moment to thank your Present Self for his/her cooperation.

I /2 minute silence.

Notice how good it feels to acknowledge your dreams and visions. Enjoy the sense of empowerment and creativity that flows as you move toward your dreams and visions. ... You have given birth to a Future Self. Know that this Self is alive and well, pulling you toward the Future you desire.

Congratulations!

1/2 minute silence.

Bid farewell to your newly created Self. Reassure him/her that you will follow through and do whatever is necessary to give this Self a chance to grow and develop. Notice how it feels to say good-bye.

1/2 minute silence.

Gently turn your attention to an awareness of your breathing and your body. Gradually return your focus back into this room and to the sounds that surround you. Feel your body in its chair. Begin to count from 1 to 5. At the count of 5, open your eyes and feel relaxed and refreshed.

1... 2... 3... 4... 5...

Work with a doll mandala before sharing your experience with others. Using colors, symbols, and/or written words, or whatever you choose, take a few moments to non-verbally express your impressions of this portion of your personhood.

Write a few sentences and thoughts in your journal. It will also be helpful to write down the first two or three steps that you have discovered.

If you are working in a group, you may form into dyads or triads to share your impressions, feelings, and experiences; take turns so that all of you have an opportunity to share. Pay particular attention to feelings, resistances, places of stuckness, or any special happenings and sensations.

Those who were not able to define an area of change and/or did not create a Future Self, might express this realization. Can you get in touch with any feelings and beliefs which could be holding you back or preventing actualization of this portion of your personhood?

EVOLUTION OF THE PSYCHE – GUIDED VISUALIZATION

Time: Approximately 1/2 hour

Introduction

In this visualization we revisit the different archetypal principals which govern the evolution of Psyche, Earthling, and humankind.[*] We start at the beginning, with Great Mother/ Goddess and physical birth. Next, we return to the world of the present, a world still ruled by Patriarchal Ego-consciousness. Patriarch bestows the gifts of psychological birth, autonomy, and independence. Evolution lovingly urges and coaxes all Consciousness to greater complexity and newly emergent possibilities. The awakening Feminine heralds the spiritual birth of a sacred, holy humanity. So let us begin your journey.

> Close your eyes and find a comfortable position. Imagine yourself resting in your favorite place, a place where you can simply be. Know you are safe in this space! Remember, you may stop this exercise at any time.

> Take three or four deep breaths at your own pace. Notice what happens to your breathing as your body and mind slow down. Continue to breathe slowly and rhythmically.

> Feel a sense of relaxation move from your toes and heels, up your calves, and into your knees. Let relaxation flow from your knees to your thighs, and into your pelvis, your hips, and your lower back... your middle back. ... Feel tension slip away from your body. Allow this sense of relaxation and well-being to move into your chest, your upper back, and shoulders. Let it gently slide down your arms—to your elbows, wrists... and down into your fingertips. Feel calmness spread over your neck, your scalp, onto your face... and over your neck and your torso. Allow your body to experience itself as deeply relaxed, limp and heavy.

> 1/2 minute of silence—Experience a state of relaxation.

> Pay attention to your breathing, and how your chest rises and falls with each inhalation and exhalation. Allow your awareness to shift from the outer world of the senses to the inner realms of consciousness.

> 1/2 minute silence

---

[*]For richer description and discussion of the Evolution of the Psyche, refer to Namasté's companion book, Once Upon ASOUL, sections 3 and 4.

We begin with humankind's emergence upon earth. Mother Earth, Father Sky, and humankind form earth's first family. All of humankind feels kinship with Universe, and basks in the companionship of fellow plants and animals. Mother Earth and Father Sky offers sanctuary, abundance, and a dwelling place. Communion and peace prevail and humanity knows it belongs.

You recognize that Communion is humanity's childhood, and that both stages are ruled by Great Mother/Goddess. When Goddess reigns, Psyche and Universe form an undifferentiated whole, and Mother and child are One. Feel the warm glow and nurturance that emanates from Great Mother/Goddess. You feel secure in her protective embrace. Great Mother/Goddess rules over an undivided house and wants you to honor the rules and cycles of her household. How does it feel to be loved so unconditionally? Experience the oneness and unity of Great Mother's love and abundance.

1 minute silence

Bravely reclaim this banished, repressed part of your consciousness. In so doing, you grow whole and in compassion. You also respond to an in-built propensity that urges you to grow, to create, and to express yourself more fully. And you feel great sadness when you realize that individuation and conscious choice cannot occur without your separation from the Matriarch/Great Mother.

1/2 minute

Suddenly, you find yourself in the midst of the mythic, legendary Fall from Paradise. It is time to leave the Garden of Eden behind. Great Mother/Goddess has been triumphantly overthrown, the emerging feminine safely repressed, and our sacred covenant with Mother Earth and Father Sky broken. Psyche, individually and collectively, has successfully slain the dragon and usurped Great Mother's throne. Now, humankind will be ruled by the Patriarch.

You breathe a sigh of relief that this important, crucial rite of passage has successfully carried you to a new level of consciousness and awareness. Take a few minutes to experience this momentous event of psychological birth. Acknowledge its significance in your personal development and evolution. Ego consciousness, under the rule of the Patriarch, will endow autonomy and independent Personhood upon you and all of humankind. "I and Thou" now dwell in your world.

1-1/2 minutes silence

Experience your psyche's internal struggle for independence and autonomy flow outward into the World of Manifestation. You grow aware that Good Mother has been transformed into Bad Mother, and Woman has became the property of Man. Do you feel a sense of loss, outrage, power, exhaltation, or?

A split occurs in Psyche as humankind moves beyond Great Mother/Goddess consciousness. You now embrace Ego consciousness, independence, individuality, and are endowed with free will, choice, and responsibility. Henceforth, You and I will experience ourselves as separate beings. What do you think will happen under Patriarch's rule and guidance?

1 minute silence

You recognize that Patriarch has severed its ties with the inner realms of existence. Humankind has left the Sacred Circle of our ancestors and now travels a linear arrow of time into a brave new world. You have a growing thirst for knowledge and experience the pace of life quicken. How does this new-found freedom and power feel to you?

1 minute silence

As Patriarch, you gradually forge a hierarchy of power and domination, and place yourself upon its apex. Your psyche now embraces the Reality Principle and only rational, linear modes of being are to be emphasized. How does it feel to be so powerful? You savor the wonders of science and technology, and shift your focus to the world of the present. You recognize that you are living in a world on the verge of insanity and collapse; chaos, uncertainty, and despair dwell in all its cities and towns. Pollution of earth's atmosphere, land, and seas is everywhere. Growing hordes of homeless and hungry citizens can be seen searching for shelter and food. Humanity's isolation and alienation from the rest of nature grows ever more visible. Clearly, we have lost our way. There is nothing wise or rational about killing portions of humanity, or desecrating our planetary home. Humanity's very survival is at stake!

1 1/2 minutes silence

You have reached an auspicious time in humanity's journey. To survive, we must learn to live in peace with one another, as well as heal Mother Earth and Father Sky. Soul urges you to let go of power, control, and domination, and to encourage a new universe to unfold. To do so, embrace Great Mother and allow your tears to flow. Mother Earth has done no wrong. She is not your enemy. Humanity must open to the compassion, love, healing, and nurturance of Great Mother, in order to survive. Care for her, as she has so lovingly cared for you. Vow to follow her cycles, restore her bounty, and protect her from further harm and abuse. Embrace Great Mother/Goddess, and reaffirm your covenant with Mother Earth and Father Sky.

1 1/2 minutes

It is important that you do not confuse Great Mother/Goddess with the emerging feminine principle. They are not the same. If you return to an earlier stage of development, and confuse the Great Mother/Goddess with the emerging Feminine, you would be inviting serious psychological regression and disturbance into your life.

Instead, choose to move forward and allow the feminine principle to emerge. You embody her ways of compassion, empathy, and relationship. Feminine stands at the interface between matter and non-matter, and serves as a gateway to the realms of Spirit. She is healer, redeemer, and resurrector. As you embrace Feminine, the Path of the Heart unfolds and beckons you forward. Will you choose the Path of the Heart?

1 minute.

To choose the Path of the Heart is to also acknowledge and heal Patriarch's shadow and thirst for unlimited dominion and power. Encourage Patriarch to release Ego-consciousness and to recognize the interdependency and relationship of all Existence. By so doing, Patriarch becomes the Masculine. Masculine ably supports and assists the emergence of your Feminine. As you awaken the Feminine, tame the Patriarch, reclaim the gifts of Great Mother/Goddess, and allow the many splits within Psyche to heal, you realize Spiritual Birth and attain greater awareness. A Sacred Marriage and partnership of Feminine and Masculine principles transpires whenever Feminine dwells within your psyche, your heart, and your world. Together, Feminine and Masculine restore wholeness, harmony, and balance to your world. Universe jubilantly allows a new era to unfold.

1 1/2 minutes silence.

And now it is time to return to the present world in which you live. You may return to these higher levels of awareness whenever Masculine and Feminine unite.

Gently return your attention to an awareness of your breathing and to your body. Gradually return your focus back into this room and to the sounds that surround you. Feel your body in its chair. Begin to count from 1 to 5. At the count of 5, open your eyes and feel relaxed and refreshed. 1... 2... 3... 4... 5...

Before you share your experience, I encourage you to work with the doll mandala. Take a few moments to non-verbally express your experience; use colors, symbols, written words, or whatever you choose. These mandalas serve as maps and symbols of today's guided journey.

You might wish to record your feelings and thoughts in a journal. Writing about your personal experiences on the Path of the Heart helps you attain and maintain a higher state of awareness. If you are working in a group, form dyads or triads to share your impressions, feelings, and experiences; take turns so that everyone has an opportunity to share. Pay particular attention to feelings, resistances, places of stuckness, or any special happenings during your visualization.

EXPLORING THE FOUR WORLDS

Personal Growth and Transformation

Each of us descends through infinite Realms of SPIRIT so that we may experience ourselves in physicality. We are encouraged to travel the Path of the Heart, which ascends through the Four Worlds, if we wish to grow and evolve to our highest potential. Your mission is to evolve and to return often to these hidden, rarefied realms of existence so that you may heal, become more whole, and reclaim SOUL. The Path of the Heart travels up and down, inward and outward, forward and backward, and all around. All directions are sacred pathways to the One We Are.

Although we speak of hidden, invisible realms of reality, it also helps to directly engage these other dimensions; in this way, theory becomes practice. I invite you to share the following guided visualization to the mysterious Realms of Spirit.

A Journey through the Four Worlds

Time: approximately 1/2 hour. This visualization may be done in its entirety or be divided into separate journeys to each of the Four Worlds. It is helpful to tape record this visualization or to have someone initially guide you through it.

This is a guided visualization for those who wish to journey upon the Path of the Heart. Find a comfortable place where you will not be disturbed or distracted. Gently close your eyes and remember you may stop at any time.

Allow your body and mind to slow down and relax. Breathe slowly and rhythmically. Feel a sense of relaxation move from your toes and heels, up your calves, and into your knees. Let relaxation flow from your knees to your thighs, and into your pelvis, your hips, and your lower back. Feel tension slip away from your body. Allow relaxation to move into your chest, your upper back, and your shoulders. Feel it gently slide down your arms... to your elbows... down into your fingertips.

Feel calmness spread over your neck, your scalp, and onto your face and back to your neck and your torso. Experience how deeply relaxed, limp, and heavy your body feels.

1/2 minute of silence—Experience stillness...

Let us begin the upward journey through the Four Worlds. Everything looks different when viewed from other worlds and dimensions. Your journey starts in the physical World of Manifestation; this is the world of your everyday existence... a world of thinking, doing, touching, feeling, hearing, tasting, and seeing.

Take a moment to tune in to your body. Experience your heart beating and follow your breath. Sense the "breath of the Invisible," the spiritual essence which flows through all forms of consciousness and existence. Notice what happens whenever you pay attention to your breath. As you relax, your body and mind relax with you. When you have completed your exploration of worlds within worlds, and levels within levels, you will again return to the world of daily existence. Allow your consciousness to freely explore the Path of the Heart.

Let your consciousness expand beyond the room in which you sit. Allow it to fill the entire building. Feel it move out to fill the city or village in which you dwell. As your consciousness continues to expand, allow it to fill the cityside, the countryside... and the oceanside. Your consciousness gradually expands beyond the city and the country, to cover oceans, mountains, deserts... until it embraces the entire world. ... As you encircle the planet with your consciousness, you become aware of your connection and relationship to everyone, everywhere, and everywhen. All are One.

As you move further out into space, allow your consciousness to flow beyond earth and to soar through the atmosphere, way beyond the stratosphere... out into the solar system, beyond our neighbors, our brother/sister planets. You are moving further out into the Milky Way galaxy. Your consciousness expands to enfold the entire universe.

As you leave the universe behind, you fill with excitement and awe. Beneath, above, and alongside our universe is an underground stream in which all consciousness is immersed. You become aware of a vast field of pulsating energy... which somehow sustains you... your loved ones, your community, your work place... your world and your universe. This loving energy endows all consciousness with a spark of the Divine. You experience the majesty... the grandeur... and the magnificent, benevolent, loving, compassionate energy that gives birth and sustains All existence. You have reached the intersection of the seen and the unseen. You are at the place where the manifest world gives way to the invisible, hidden domains of the unmanifest Realms of Spirit. Allow the awe and mystery of this experience to flow through your being. Encourage your consciousness to merge with this sacred ground of awareness. Do not be afraid. Spirit will not harm you.

1/2 minute silence.

You are now approaching the World of Formation, a dimension of endless potential, infinite possibilities, and magnificent variation. You visit this realm during reverie, altered states of consciousness, and especially at Dream-Time. This is an eternal, timeless realm in which SOUL stores myriad plans, blueprints, life scripts, and designs for your own personal growth and evolution. Here you will find all the riches SOUL wishes to bestow upon you. ... You may even glimpse your destiny.

1/2 minute silence.

Look about the World of Formation. Do you see an idea, a solution, a song, a relationship... which you wish to manifest in the World of Physicality upon your return? Can you find a special gift from SOUL?

1/2 minute.

The World of Formation is a world filled with archetypes and angels, with gods and demons; it is a collective world, as well as the gateway to SOUL. If you have discovered a gift, ask that it be wrapped for you, so that you may take it with you when you return to the World of Manifestation. If you are experiencing a problem, you might ask to see possible solutions. Take responsibility and choose the solution you feel will be most helpful. In order to actualize the potential of the World of Formation, you must be willing to fully engage and interact with it. No event or object may enter your physical world unless it receives your invitation to become manifest.

Now bid the World of Formation good-bye and enter the World of Creation. This is a vast, spacious, timeless domain of great generativity and creation. Here you observe the endless Dance of Shiva as energy becomes matter and matter is transformed into energy. This is the birthing place of earthly consciousness. It is here that each being receives the spark of the Divine. This is where you and I begin. The World of Creation is the dwelling place of SOUL, and your ancestral home. ...

You will only briefly glimpse this world, for it is a world of transcendence and subtlety... of energy, majesty, and grandeur. You may only remain a moment or two... just long enough to get a taste. ... Here manifest and unmanifest SELVES unite... and you become Whole.

But this is not ALL THAT IS. Beyond the Worlds of Genesis and Creation lie infinite worlds within worlds which ascend to the World of Emanation and the Realms of SPIRIT... the Void... the Abyss... the emptiness and stillness of ALL... the dwelling place of Infinite Consciousness. ...

Allow your Consciousness a momentary glimpse and then let go... this realm is too subtle and too rarefied to remain for very long. Here past, present, and future exist as part of a seamless, unbroken whole. This is All.

1/2 minute silence.

Now it is time to return to earth. Bid the invisible, hidden, unmanifest realms of Spirit good-bye. You may return to these multitudinous dimensions of awareness another time. As you descend into the World of Creation, you embrace SOUL. All portions of SELF are One. Together they forge a unity.

As you leave SOUL and the World of Creation, you again enter a more dense realm of possibilities... of maybes... if I want, I can. The World of Formation is indeed a magical domain. It gives rise to all that exists in the World of Manifestation; the ideals, forms, shapes, scripts, patterns of your everyday world of space-time and matter are found in this domain.

As you approach the physical universe, you again hear and see normally. You sense the vastness and enormity of outer space. Time and gravity pull you toward your special corner of Universe. Returning from the very edge of Universe, traveling through dark matter and galaxies and solar systems... you near your planetary home in the Milky Way. You have traveled light years of time. Gradually, find your way to the third planet around our sun. This beautiful blue and white planet is earth. You are home. .... Slowly, descend through the stratosphere and the atmosphere, layer by layer... until you see nations, cities, and towns. Just ahead is your home and your family.

Gently return your attention to your breathing and to your body. Gradually return your focus back into this room and to the sounds that surround you. Feel your body in its chair. Begin to count from 1 to 5. At the count of five, open your eyes and feel relaxed and refreshed. 1... 2... 3... 4... 5...

I encourage you to work with a mandala of the Four Worlds before you share your experience. Using colors, symbols, written words, or whatever you choose, take a few moments to non-verbally express your impressions of your journey through the Four Worlds. The Four Worlds mandala serves as a symbol of today's visit.

Write a few sentences and thoughts in your journal. If you are working in a group, form into dyads or triads to share your impressions, feelings, and experiences; take turns so that everyone has an opportunity to share.

Exploring the mystical Four Worlds personally challenges you to grow and to evolve. As Self and Soul embrace, wholeness replaces fragmentation, and inner peace jubilantly fills your world.

THE FOUR WORLDS

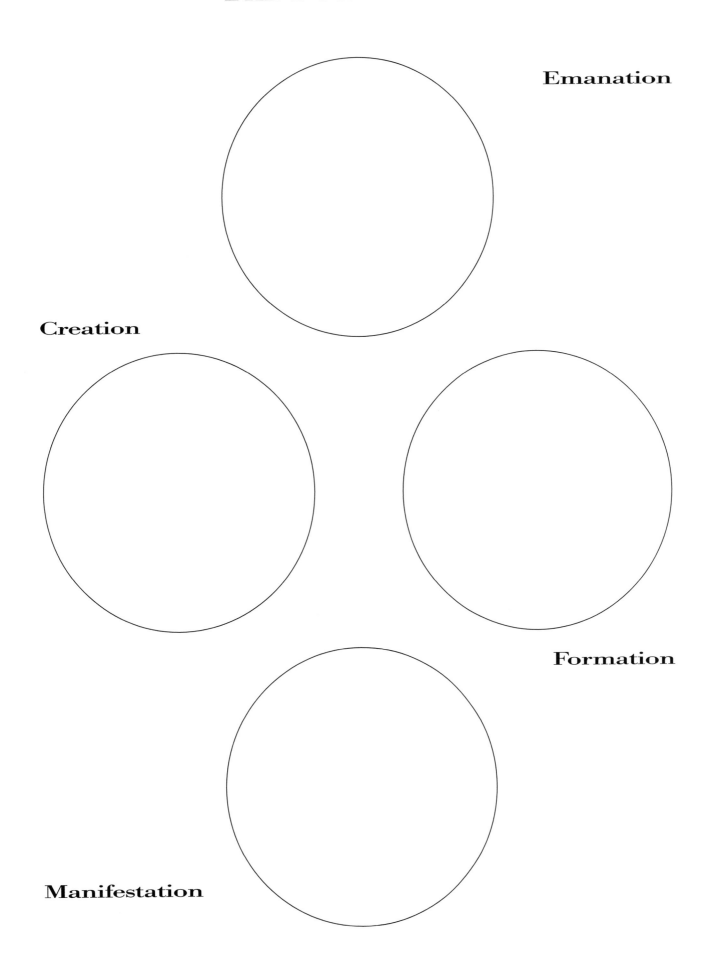

Emanation

Creation

Formation

Manifestation

PEACE

Humanity must encounter its inner demons and rage in order to heal. We must stop warring with one another and learn how to live in peace. Yet, humanity continues to experience the global escalation of war. As population expands beyond earth's ability to feed and sustain us, pestilence, famine, and war increase.

The paths of war do not discriminate; it matters not whose child or grandchild dies. War seeks only the illusion of victory. Indeed, there is neither triumph nor honor in human slaughter and war. Rich or poor, young or old, black, yellow, red, white, or brown, all will die if we do not transform our ways of violence and war to those of peace. Humankind is trapped in an endless cycle of hate, rage, and destruction. War only begets war; it has always been so!

Yet there is cause for hope and celebration. Earth people have witnessed the end of the cold war and the toppling of the Berlin Wall. Nations strive to reunite East and West with North and South. Many countries are struggling with the awesome responsibilities of newly gained freedom, choosing democracy and new possibilities, rather than returning to ways of dictatorship and war. Growing numbers of individuals are transcending the boundaries of an ego-centric Self to embrace wholeness. Innovative paradigms and global reform reflect humankind's courage and maturity. These are true victories for humankind. As Earthlings evolve beyond violence and greed, a peaceful world becomes a tangible possibility.

Affirming Peace

Mission: Gather friends and family together to affirm peace as essential to all life.

Can you imagine inviting your family and friends to a Celebration for Peace? Ask everyone who attends to share their hopes and visions for a peaceful universe. Another idea is to ask your guests to bring an offering of peace to your ceremony. As you sit or stand in a circle, each person gets an opportunity to speak about their chosen gift and its healing properties. At the conclusion of this sacred ceremony, ask your guests to proclaim "May Peace Prevail on Earth" in many of earth's languages. What else are you willing to do to bring peace into your world?

Guided Visualization on Peace

Have you ever wondered what a world at peace would be like? The first few moments are easy to imagine. But once crime, violence, bombs, and war have been eradicated, how does the world proceed? It is a profoundly different world from the one we presently know. Let us try to imagine a world at peace.

Close your eyes and find a comfortable position. I will guide you into a relaxed, aware state. I invite you to consider a world at peace. You might choose one special area of interest to focus upon, such as education, family, career, population, the biosphere... or you might wish to look at the whole web of life offered by a peace-loving world.

I invite you to feel peace. I invite you to taste peace.
I invite you to hear peace. I invite you to see peace.
I invite you to Be Peace.

When you are ready, return your awareness to this room. Open your eyes and awaken to deep peace.

Creating a Global Community for Peace

Millennium Action Teams and Peace and Environmental Teams (MATs and PETs)

Peace on Earth and Peace with Earth are about personal transformation and action taken by thousands, hopefully millions, of individuals over the next millennium and beyond. Action to improve the health of our families, our societies, and our world is desperately needed.

We are faced with the greatest threats our planet has ever known. Let us use the threat of impending disaster as an incentive to take the steps necessary to resolve these seemingly insurmountable problems.

The year 2000 serves as a powerful archetypal symbol—the beginning of a new millennium. It is imperative that we harness the power of this critical time in our planet's history and channel it into meaningful Action through education, inspiration, and implementation.

Many of these goals can be accomplished through the creation of Millennium Action Teams (MATs) and Peace and Environmental Teams (PETs). Such teams, composed of 5-10 individuals sharing similar visions and goals, will, together, develop and augment activities to foster a sustainable peace and a healthy environment for humanity's continued survival upon earth. MATs and PETs can serve as a "living laboratory," allowing individuals and groups to explore, develop, and apply existing and newly created solutions to the urgent problems and challenges awaiting humankind. MATs and PETs regenerate the spirit of service and help humanity to live in peace.

How to Form PETs and MATs

Pick a global issue, one that you are especially concerned about. It might be toxic waste, nuclear power, education, alternative healing techniques, conflict resolution, human rights, parenting skills, soil erosion, etc. Anything that concerns or interests you is an appropriate choice. Define an area within this issue. Be careful not to make your project so big that you will quickly become discouraged and quit.

Invite 4-7 individuals with a similar concern to join your team. Choose one person to be coordinator so that things will continue to move smoothly. In some groups, everyone can have the same academic expertise, e.g. a team concerned with teaching skills might be composed of all teachers. Perhaps your project requires the skills of many professions. For example, a global project may require the skills of a secretary, a legal expert, a financial advisor as well as an international expert. You decide what type of team will work best for you.

Determine your goals and target dates, and designate a person to call upon when difficulties arise. Keep your team apprised of your efforts, problems, and progress. Remember, you are a member of a team; everyone is counting on you to do your part. Let them know that you also are counting on them to do theirs. The fate of Mother Earth and humanity rests upon the decisions and actions we individually and collectively choose.

Humanity has the power to cause great devastation, destruction, and pain; we also have the power to create great beauty, harmony, and fulfillment. Humanity is presently dwelling within a sacred chrysalis. A new form of human being is beginning to awaken. An entirely new form of Consciousness is emerging. Will our world support and sustain our new spiritual identity?

The true alchemy of the SOUL is the reconciliation of light and dark within. When that transformation is achieved, we will no longer need to blame or to hurt one another. Let us move from fear to trust, from harm to harmony, to become a people who make peace instead of war!

As you contemplate humanity's future, it is helpful to think about the world you wish to inhabit in the coming millennium. How do you envision humankind's future? "2070 A.D.—The Wisdom Age" is my personal hope for humankind.

2070 A.D.—THE WISDOM AGE

The world of 2070 A.D. is a vision of a new era. It is a world filled with hope, promise, and opportunity. Its people have achieved a sustainable economy and a sustainable ecology. They live in balance and harmony with the cycles and rhythms of the cosmos, and respect all forms of life and consciousness.

The world of 2070 A. D. is founded upon the Sacred Marriage of masculine and feminine elements in Psyche, and a new spiritual covenant with Universe. The citizens of 2070 A.D. know the inner paths of the psyche. They are equally at home in the worlds of matter and non-matter, for they have long recognized that they are One.

Balance in population, food supply, and energy resources ensures that every child is a wanted child and is properly cared for. Parenting is considered the most noble of vocations. The "Mothering Ones" are esteemed and cherished along with the children they nurture.

More mature and humane solutions to conflict and discord have been discovered and promoted. The world of 2070 A.D. knows no honor, glory, or profit through war.

Elders are valued for their abilities and experiences. Their presence and their gifts enrich the entire community. The Wisdom age is the culmination and gift of a life well-lived. Advancing age affords an opportunity to more fully embrace and explore the inner paths of transcendence.

Creativity and the willingness to grow are prized attributes in the land of 2070 A.D. People of all ages are encouraged to create, to risk, to fail, and to succeed. Essentially, they are free simply to be whomever they are. Black, white, yellow, red, or brown, all citizens are equal and all are cherished. This is a world that honors and respects diversity. Value fulfillment is everyone's privilege; it is freely offered to all who dwell in this peaceful realm.

2070 A.D. inspires and encourages its citizens to become dreamers, seers, and prophets. They have learned that their dreams and future emanate from the invisible archetypal realms of the psyche, and beyond. The seeds of inspiration and wisdom are transmitted to 2070 A.D. through its visionaries and enlightened ones. No society can long endure without the arts, music, literature, and visions that reflect its highest potential. Archetypal 2070 A.D. dwells in the hearts and Souls of humankind. It symbolizes our promise and our birthright.

The enlightened, peaceful land of 2070 A.D. sharply contrasts with the shadowy, dark world we presently know. In our current world, we experience violence, despair, greed, hate, abuse, violation of human rights, and the desecration of Mother Earth. It seems unlikely, even futile, to believe that we could ever realize and attain such a reality.

We are like the people in Plato's Cave[*29] seeing only the shadows and hints of another reality. Like Plato's people, we are faced with an awesome choice. We can refuse to believe and change or, instead, we can embrace the light and leave our darkness behind. 2070 A.D. already exists within the realms of possibility. It is humankind's destiny and future. Carpe diem. Dare we seize the opportunity?

Humankind is approaching the next evolution of Consciousness and perception that corresponds to Reconciliation and Union. It urges us beyond the limitations of gender, stereotyped roles, and the prejudice against race or creed. It imparts dignity and respect to all human beings. In the life cycle of ASELF, it represents the choices and responsibilities of conscious adulthood.

Recognition that Psyche continues to develop throughout one's entire lifespan implies that humankind might yet realize more periods of chaos and uncertainty as our species experiences middle-age, and as we accrue the wisdom and grace of an ancient people. Each stage in Psyche's cycle of life guides and directs our continuing sojourn upon earth.

Humanity must successfully navigate and accomplish an inner reconciliation of masculine and feminine principles in order to realize its fuller potential and to embrace the One and the Many. Transpersonal Human will soon dwell upon earth. The caterpillar is transforming itself into a butterfly. When the metamorphosis is complete, we will know the One We Are, consciously, for the very first time.

ASELF's Prayer

> ASELF awakened with a sigh,
> 　　She yearned to dwell in 2070 A.D.
> She knew that you and I
> 　　would determine its reality.
>
> ASELF beseeched one and all
> 　　to heed SPIRIT's Soulful call.
> She encouraged us to awaken and become whole
> 　　Humankind would soon embrace ASOUL.

Let us take ASELF's sacred prayer into our next meditation. Use this opportunity to create your own vision for the new millennium.

---

[*]"The dwellers in the den see only the shadow of puppets, which are themselves only imitations of living things. That is, they see only the appearance of material things, not the true nature." Plato's *The Republic,* pp. 398–399.

The World of 2070 A.D.—A Guided Visualization

Time: Approximately 1/2 hour.

Close your eyes and find a comfortable position. Imagine yourself resting in a favorite place, a place where you can simply be. Know you are safe in this space! Remember, you may stop this exercise at any time.

Take three or four deep breaths at your own pace. Feel your body and mind slow down and relax. Continue to breathe slowly and rhythmically. ...

Feel a sense of relaxation move from your toes and heels, up your calves and into your knees. Let relaxation flow from your knees to your thighs and into your pelvis, your hips and your lower back, your middle back. Feel tension slip away from your body. Allow this sense of relaxation and well-being to move into your chest, your upper back, and shoulders. Let it gently slide down your arms—to your elbows, wrists, and down into your fingertips. Feel calmness spread over your neck, your scalp, onto your face... and over your neck and your torso. Allow your body to experience itself as deeply relaxed, limp, and heavy.

1/2 minute of silence - Experience a state of relaxation.

Pay attention to your breathing; watch your chest rise and fall with each inhalation and exhalation. Encourage your awareness to move from the outer world to the inner realms of Consciousness.

Imagine that you are approaching a pathway of ten stones. As you step upon the first stone, feel your Self growing more relaxed... step on the second... move on to the third step. Walk onto stone four, followed by stone five and then six. You will see a sunny meadow just ahead. Move on to steps seven, eight, and nine... and then on to the tenth stone. Notice a sense of excitement and anticipation. Do not hurry. Just find a comfortable place in this sunny meadow... and relax.

As you sit quietly, you may see someone approaching you... your visitor may be an angel, an animal, an insect, an archetype, or a guide. See if a particular being reveals itself to you. ... Do not censor this guide, even if it is someone unexpected. Just stay centered and calm... honor this sacred occasion.

Some of you may not see anyone; simply acknowledge what does or does not happen. It is alright. You may feel joy and exhilaration. Sit quietly and wait to see who appears. When a being arrives, greet it and thank it for coming. You might ask what the world of 2070 A.D. is like... or whether humankind will survive. Accept your first thoughts as your answer.

1 1/2 minutes silence.

Some of you may receive an answer to your questions .You may or may not like this answer or even understand it. Simply allow it to be. Perhaps you have your own vision of the world of 2070 A.D.

Permit your yearnings for survival and Transpersonal specieshood to stir your heart and Soul. ...What are your deepest hopes and dreams?

2 minutes silence.

Let us repeat ASELF's Prayer once more.

ASELF's PRAYER

ASELF awakened with a sigh,
    She yearned to dwell in 2070 A.D.
She knew that you and I
    would determine its reality.

ASELF beseeched one and all
    to heed SPIRIT's Soulful call.
She encouraged us to awaken and become whole
    Humankind would soon embrace ASOUL.

May peace and harmony dwell in our present world as well.

As you leave the world of 2070 A.D. behind, take a moment to thank your visitor for coming. Let this being know how much you appreciate this visit.

1/2 minute silence.

Notice how good it feels to acknowledge your dreams and visions. Recognize the growing sense of empowerment and creativity you attain whenever you move toward your dreams and visions. ... Let us make the world of 2070 A.D. a reality for our children, our children's children, and our children's grandchildren. ... Let us make "Peace" a way of life!

1/2 minute silence.

Gently return your attention to an awareness of your breathing and to your body. Gradually return your focus back into this room and to the sounds that surround you. Feel your body in its chair. Begin to count from 1 to 5. At the count of 5, open your eyes and feel relaxed and refreshed. 1... 2... 3... 4... 5...

Before you share your experience, I encourage you to work with the global mandala. Take a few moments to non-verbally express your experience; use colors, symbols, written words, or whatever you choose. The World mandala symbolize today's journey.

Record your feelings and thoughts in your journal. It is also helpful to write your personal vision for the world of 2070 A.D. so that you can make it a reality.

If you are working in a group, form into dyads or triads to share your impressions, feelings, and experiences; take turns so that everyone has an opportunity to share. Pay particular attention to feelings, resistances, places of stuckness, and any special happenings during your visualization.

ENLIGHTENMENT

Transformation is a lifelong challenge as well as a humbling process. It cannot be hurried. Every risk bestows deeper insight and increased awareness, until one day, you come to the realization that there is no end to your journey. There is never a time when you will know it all. You grow aware that any idea of completion is only an illusion. Slowly, perhaps reluctantly, you release your attachment to "perfection," and gradually accept your Self and your humanity. Each destination becomes a new beginning; there are still more levels of Self, Psyche, and Soul yet to explore. Spirit's sacred call invites you to journey from life to Life and Self to SELF. The Path of the Heart is an endless voyage of discovery and unfolding. Namasté!

WORLD OF 2070 A.D.

NOTES

1. J. Campbell in P. Russell, *The White Hole In Time* (New York, Harper San Francisco, 1992), p. 174.
2. W. Maathai, in *As Above, So Below* (Los Angeles, Jeremy P. Tarcher, Inc., 1992), p. 262.
3. Kenya, in *Seeds of Peace* (Philadelphia, New Society Publishers, 1987), p. 118.
4. S. Colegrave, *Uniting Heaven & Earth* (Los Angeles, Jeremy P. Tarcher, Inc., 1979), p. 76.
5. J. and R. Woolger, in *As Above, So Below* (Los Angeles, Jeremy P. Tarcher, Inc. 1992), p. 160.
6. Michael Washburn, *The Ego and the Dynamic Ground,* 2nd. Ed. (S.U.N.Y. Press, Albany, 1995), p. 14.
7. Stephen Schutz, Ph.D. and Susan Polis Schutz, *Love in 5-D Stereograms* (Blue Mountain Press, Boulder, 1994).
8. Richard L. Gregory (Ed.), *The Oxford Companion to Mind* (Oxford University Press, Oxford, 1987), pp. 340 and 345.
9. C. G. Jung, *Dreams, Memories, Reflections* (New York, Pantheon Books, 1973), p. 3.
10. Carol Pearson, *The Hero Within: Six Archetypes We Live By* (Harper & Row, New York, 1987) and *Awakening The Heros Within* (Harper-San Francisco, New York, 1991).
11. Heita Copony, *Mystery of Mandalas,* Quest Books (Theosophical Publishing House, Wheaton, 1989).
12. T.W. Graham Solomons, *Fundamentals of Organic Chemistry* (John Wiley & Sons, New York, 1982), pp. 365-367.
13. J. S. Bergan & Str. M. Schwan, *Love: A Guide for Prayer* (Winona, St. Mary's Press, 1985).
14. D. L. Fleming, S. J., *The Spiritual Exercises of St. Ignatius,* A Literal Translation and A Contemporary Reading (St. Louis, The Institute of Jesuit Sources, 1978).
15. Thomas E. Mails, *Secret Native American PATHWAYS* (Council Oak Books, Oklahoma, no date).
16. Sun Bear, Wabun Wind, Crysalis Mulligan, *Dancing with the Wheel* (Fireside, Simon & Schuster, New York, 1991).
17. Ojibuay prayer, North America.
18. Ecclesiastes III, 1-4.
19. Norman Cousins, *Anatomy of an Illness* (W.W. Norton & Company, New York, 1979).
20. Paula B. Doress-Worters and Diana Laskin Siegal, *The New Ourselves, Growing Older, Women Aging with Knowledge and Power* (Touchstone, Simon and Schuster, New York, 1994), p. 418.
21. *"To Those I Love and Those Who Love Me."* a poem, anonymous.
22. Alexander Pope, *Essay on Criticism, Part II,* line 325. in John Bartlett, *Familiar Quotations* (Little, Brown and Company, Boston, 1955).
23. Zsuzsanna E. Budapest, *The Grandmother of Time* (Harper-San Francisco, New York, 1989).
24. I. Progoff, *Jung, Synchronicity and Human Destiny* (New York, Delta Books, 1975).
25. A. Roddick, in *As Above, So Below* (Los Angeles, Jeremy P. Tarcher, Inc., 1992), p. 288.
26. R. Campbell, M. D., in *Chop Wood, Carry Water* (Los Angeles, Jeremy P. Tarcher, Inc., 1984), p. 91.
27. J. Gardner, *Self Renewal* (New York, Sterling Lord Literistic, 1964).
28. T. Hansel
29. Plato, *The Republic* (Roslyn, Walter J. Black, Inc. 1942), pp. 398–399.

SELECTED BIBLIOGRAPHY

Jeanne Achterberg Ph.D., Barbara Dossey, R.N., M.S., FAAN, and Leslie Kolkmeier, R.N., M.Ed. *Rituals of Healing: Using Imagery for Health and Wellness* (Bantam Books, New York, 1994).

Larry Dossey, M.D. *Healing Words: The Power of Prayer and The Practice of Medicine* (Harper-Collins, New York, 1993).

Thich Nhat Hanh, *The Blooming of a Lotus: Guided Meditation Exercises for Healing and Transformation* (Beacon Press, Boston, 1993).

Caryle Hirshberg & Mark Ian Barasch, *Remarkable Recovery* (Riverhead Books, New York, 1995).

Andrew Weil, M.D., *Spontaneous Healing* (Knopf, New York, 1995).

Fred Alan Wolf, Ph.D., *The Dreaming Universe* (Simon & Schuster, New York, 1994).